Brander Matthews

**Americanisms and Briticisms**

With other Essays on other isms

Brander Matthews

**Americanisms and Briticisms**
*With other Essays on other isms*

ISBN/EAN: 9783337176174

Printed in Europe, USA, Canada, Australia, Japan

Cover: Foto ©ninafisch / pixelio.de

More available books at **www.hansebooks.com**

# AMERICANISMS AND BRITICISMS

## WITH OTHER ESSAYS ON OTHER ISMS

BY

BRANDER MATTHEWS

NEW YORK

HARPER AND BROTHERS

MDCCCXCII

50549

TO

# THOMAS R. LOUNSBURY

## YALE UNIVERSITY

*My dear Lounsbury,—In reading over the proof-sheets of these pages, I have happened on your name more often than I thought I had written it, and yet not so often by once as I wish to write it. So I set it here, in the forefront of this little book, to bear witness that much of what may be good in these essaylets of mine is due to help given by you, either directly by word of mouth or indirectly by the printed page. And that is why I take pleasure now in subscribing myself as*

*Yours gratefully,*

BRANDER MATTHEWS

Columbia College
*September,* 1892

# CONTENTS

|  | Page |
|---|---|
| AMERICANISMS AND BRITICISMS. . . | 1 |
| AS TO "AMERICAN SPELLING" . | 32 |
| THE LITERARY INDEPENDENCE OF THE UNITED STATES . . . . . | 60 |
| THE CENTENARY OF FENIMORE COOPER . | 89 |
| IGNORANCE AND INSULARITY . . . | 103 |
| THE WHOLE DUTY OF CRITICS . . . | 114 |
| THREE AMERICAN ESSAYISTS. . . . | 135 |
| DISSOLVING VIEWS : | |
| I. OF MARK TWAIN'S BEST STORY . | 151 |
| II. OF A NOVEL OF M. ZOLA'S . | 161 |
| III. OF WOMEN'S NOVELS . . . . | 169 |
| IV. OF TWO LATTERDAY HUMORISTS . | 177 |

ON a novel written in the last decade but one of the nineteenth century by an Australian lady in collaboration with a member of Parliament, one of the characters stops another "to ask for the explanation of this or that Australian phrase," wondering whether "it would be better to give the English meaning of each word after the word itself, and to keep on repeating it all through, or would it do to put a footnote once for all, or how would it do to have a little glossary at the end?" As it happens, oddly enough, the authors of *The Ladies' Gallery* have not themselves done any one of these things; and therefore, if we chance to read their fiction, we are left to grope for ourselves when in the first two chapters we are told of "the wild howling of the *dingoes* in the

1

*scrub,*" and when we learn that the hero had "eaten his evening meal—*damper* and a hard junk of *wallabi* flesh "—while his "*billy* of tea was warming." Then we are informed that "he had arranged a bed with his blankets, his *swag* for a pillow," and that he wished for a good mate to share his watch, or even "a black *tracker* upon whom he could depend as a scout." We are told also that this hero, who "was not intended to *grub* along," hears a call in the night, and he reflects "that a black fellow would not *cou-ee* in that way." Later he cuts up "a *fig* of tobacco;" he says "we can *yarn* now;" he speaks of living on wild plums and *bandicoot;*" and he makes mention of "a certain *newchum.*" From the context we may fairly infer that this last term is the Australian equivalent of the Western *tenderfoot;* but who shall explain the meaning of *damper* and *dingoes, cou-ee* and *bandicoot?* And why have *scrub* and *billy, grub* and *fig,* taken on new meanings, as though they had suffered a sea-change in the long voyage around the Cape or through the canal?

As yet, so far as I know, no British critic has raised a cry of alarm against the coming degradation of the English language by the invasion of Australian-isms. It can hardly be doubted, however, that the necessities of a new civilization will force the Australian to the making of many a new word to define new conditions. As the San Francisco *hoodlum* is different from the New York *loafer*, so the Melbourne *larrikin* has differentiated himself from the London *rough*, and in due season a term had to be developed to denote this differentiation. There are also not a few Canadian phrases to be collected by the curious; and the exiles in India have evolved a vocabulary of their own by a frequent adoption of native words, which makes difficult the reading of certain of Mr. Rudyard Kipling's earlier tales. To recall these things is but to recognize that the same causes are at work in Canada, in India, and in Australia as have been acting in the United States. It remains to be seen whether the British critic will show the same intolerance towards the colonial and dependent Australian and Canadian that he has been wont to show towards the independent American. The controversy, when it comes, is one at which the American will look on with disinterested amusement, remembering that those laugh best who laugh last, and that Dean Alford omitted from the later editions of his dogmatic discussion of the *Queen's English* a passage which was prominent in the first edition, issued in 1863, during the war of the rebellion, and which animadverted on the process of deterioration that the Queen's English had undergone at the hands of the Americans. " Look at those phrases," he cried, "which so amuse us in their speech and books, at their reckless exaggeration and contempt for congruity, and then compare the character and history of the nation—its blunted sense of moral obligation and duty to man, its open disregard of conventional right where aggrandizement is to be obtained, and I may now say, its reckless and fruitless maintenance of the most cruel and unprincipled war in the history of the world." Time can be relied on to quash an indictment against a nation, and we Americans should be sorry to think that there are to-day in England any of those who in 1863 sympathized with the Dean of Canterbury, and who are not now heartily ashamed of their attitude then.

Owing, it may be, to the consciousness of strength, which is a precious result of the war the British clergyman denounced thus eloquently, the last tie of colonialism which bound us to the mother-country is broken. We know now that the mother-tongue is a heritage and not a loan. It is ours to use as we needs must. In America there is no necessity to plead for the right of the Americanism to exist. The cause is won. No American writer worth his salt would think of withdrawing a word or of apologizing for a phrase because it was not current within sound of Bow Bells. The most timid of American authoresses has no doubt as to her use of *railroad, conductor, grade,* and to *switch,* despite her possible knowledge that in British usage the equivalents of these words are *railway, guard, gradient,* and to *shunt.* On the contrary, in fact, there is visible now and again, especially on the part of the most highly cultivated writers, an obvious delight in grasping an indigenous word racy of the soil. There is many an American expression of a pungent freshness which authors, weary of an outworn vocabulary, seize eagerly. It may be a new word, but it would not be in accord with our traditions to refuse naturalization to a welcome new-comer; or it may be a survival flourishing here in our open fields, although long since rooted out of the trim island garden on the other side of the Atlantic, and in such case we use it unhesitatingly to-day as our forefathers used it in the past, "following," as Lowell remarks, " the fashion of our ancestors, who unhappily could bring over no English better than Shakespeare's."

In the preface to the first edition of his dictionary, issued in 1825, Noah Webster declared that although in America "the body of the language is the same as in England, and it is desirable to perpetuate that sameness, yet some differences must exist," since " language is the expression of ideas, and if the people of one country cannot preserve an identity of ideas " with the people of another country, they are not likely to retain an absolute identity of language; and Webster had no difficulty in showing that differences of physical and political conditions had already in his day, only half a century after the Revolution, and when the centre of population was still close to the Atlantic seaboard, produced differences of speech. It is too much to expect, perhaps, that the British critic shall look at this Yankee independence from our point of view. Professor Lounsbury tells us in his admirable biography that in Fenimore Cooper's time the attitude of the Englishman towards the American "in the most favorable cases . . . was supercilious and patronizing, an attitude which never permits the nation criticising to understand the nation criticised." Things have changed for the better since Cooper was almost alone in his stalwart Americanism, but the arrogance which General Braddock of his Majesty's army showed towards Colonel Washington of the Virginia contingent survives here and there in Great Britain, even though another dean sits in Dr. Alford's stall in Canterbury Cathedral; it prompted a British novelist not long ago to be offensively impertinent to an American lady (*Athenæum*, September 1, 1888), and it allowed Lord Wolseley to insult the memory of Robert E. Lee with ignorant praise. It finds expression in a passage like the following from a *Primer of English Composition*, by Mr. John Nichols: "Americanisms, as ' Britisher,' ' skedaddle,' and the peculiar use of 'clever,' 'calculate,' 'guess, 'reckon,' etc., with the mongrel speech adopted by some humorists, are only admissible in satirical pictures of American manners" (p. 35). When we read an assertion of this sort, we are reduced to believe that it must be the dampness of the British climate which has thus rusted the hinges of British manners.

Far more often than we could wish can we hear the note of lofty condescension in British discussion of the peculiarities of other races. When Englishmen are forced to compare themselves with men of any other country, no doubt it must be difficult for them not to plume themselves on their superior virtue. But modesty is also a virtue, and if this were more often cultivated in Great Britain, the French, for example, would have fewer occasions for making pointed remarks about *la morgue britannique*. Even the gentle Thackeray —if the excursus may be forgiven—is not wholly free from this failing. In spite of his familiarity with French life and French art, he could not quite divest himself of his British pride, and of the intolerance which accompanies it, and therefore we find him recording that M. de Florac confided gayly to Mr. Clive New-come the reason why he preferred the coffee at the hotel to the coffee at the great café "with a *duris urgéns in rebūs égcstsās!* pronounced in the true French manner" (*Newcomes,* chapter xxviii.). But how should a Frenchman pronounce Latin ?—like an Englishman, perhaps ? When even the kindly Thackeray is capable of a sneering insularity of this sort, it is small wonder that the feeling of the French towards the British is well expressed in the final line of the quatrain inscribed over the gate at Compiègne through which Joan Darc went to her capture :

"Tous ceux-là d'Albion n'ont faict le bien jamais !"

And we are reminded of the English lady who was taken to see Mr. Jefferson's performance of Rip Van Winkle, and who liked it very much indeed, but thought it such a pity that the actor had so strong an American accent !

" Ignorance of his neighbor is the character of the typical John Bull," says Mr. R. L. Stevenson, who also declares that "the Englishman sits apart bursting with pride and ignorance." What a Scot has written a Yankee may quote. And the quotation has pertinence here in view of the fact that in the last century the English were just as keen against Scotticisms and Hibernicisms, and just as bitter, as they have been in this century against Americanisms, and as they may be in the next against Australianisms. Macaulay asserted that there were in *Marmion* and in *Waverley* "Scotticisms at which a London apprentice would laugh;" and there are to be seen in the English newspapers now and again petty attacks on the style and vocabulary of American authors of distinction, which it is perhaps charitable to credit to London apprentices. One of these it was no doubt who began a review of Mr. Brownell's subtle and profound study of *French Traits* with the statement that "the language most depressing to the educated Englishman is the language of the cultured American." Probably the small sword will always be exasperating to those who cling to the boxing-glove.

When a London apprentice laughs at the Scotticisms of the North Briton, and

when the London *Athenæum* is depressed
by the language of cultured Americans,
there is to be discovered behind the
laugh and the scoff an assumption that
any departure from the usage which obtains in London is most deplorable. The
laugh and the scoff are the outward and
visible signs of an inward and spiritual belief that the Londoner is the sole guardian and trustee of the English language.
But this is a belief for which there is no
foundation whatever. The English language is not bankrupt that it needs to
have a receiver appointed; it is quite
capable of minding its own business without the care of a committee of Englishmen. If indeed a guardian were necessary, what Englishman would it be who
would best preserve our pure English—the
shepherd of Dorset or the miner of Nor-
thumberland, the Yorkshire man or the
cockney? If it is not the London apprentice who is to set the standard, but
the Englishman of breeding, it is hard to
discover the ground whereon this Englishman can claim superiority of taste or
knowledge over the other educated men
to whom English is the mother-tongue,
whether they were born in Scotland, Ire-

land, or America, in Australia, India, or Canada.

The fallacy of the Englishman, be he London apprentice or contributor to the *Athenæum*, is that he erects a merely personal standard in the use of our language. He compares the English he finds in the novels of a Scotchman or in the essays of an American with that which he hears about him daily in London, animadverting upon every divergence from this local British usage as a departure from the strict letter of the law which governs our language. It is, of course, unfair to suggest that a parochial self-satisfaction underlies this utilization of personal experience as the sole test of linguistic propriety; but the procedure is amusingly illogical.

The cockney has no monopoly of good English if even he has his full portion. The Englishman in England is but the elder brother of the Anglo-Saxon elsewhere; and by no right of primogeniture does he control the language which is our birthright. Noah Webster, in the preface from which quotation has already been made, remarked that American authors had a tendency to write " the language in

its genuine idiom," and he asserted that
" in this respect Franklin and Washington, whose language is their hereditary
mother-tongue, unsophisticated by modern grammar, present as pure models of
genuine English as Addison or Swift."
It may be doubted whether English is
now more vigorously spoken or better
understood in London than in New York
or in Melbourne; but it is indisputable
that the student detects in the ordinary
speech of the Englishman many a lapse
from the best usage.  This contaminat-
ing of the well of English undefiled is not
to be defended because it is due to Englishmen who happen to live in England.
A blunder made in Great Britain is to be
stigmatized as a Briticism, and it is to be
avoided by those who take thought of
their speech just as though the impropri-
ety were a Scotticism or a Hibernicism,
an Americanism or an Australianism.
When a locution of the London apprentice is not in accord with the principles
of the language, there is no prejudice in
its favor because it happened to arise
beside the Thames rather than on the
shores of the Hudson or by the banks of
the St. Lawrence.

Of Briticisms there are as many and as
worthy of collection and collocation as
were the most of the Americanisms the
all-embracing Bartlett gathered into his
dictionary. Indeed, if a Scot or a Yankee
were to prepare a glossary of Briticisms
on the ample scale adopted by Mr. Bartlett, and with the same generous hospi-
tality, the result would surprise no one
more than the Englishman. We should
find in its pages many a word and phrase
and turn of speech common enough in
England and quite foreign to the best
usage of those who speak English—Briticisms as worthy of reproof as the worst
specimen of "the mongrel speech adopted
by some humorists in America." These
are to be sought rather in the written language than in oral speech, though there
are Briticisms a-plenty in the talk of the
Londoner, from the suppression of the
initial *h* among the masses to the dropping
of the final *g* among the classes. Of a truth,
precision of speech is not frequent in
London, and not seldom the delivery of
the Englishman of education nowadays
may fairly be called slovenly. As I recall
the list of those whom I have heard use
the English language with mingled ease

and elegance, I find fewer Englishmen
than either Scotchmen or Americans.
Quintilian tells us that an old Athenian
woman called the eloquent Theophrastus
a stranger, and declared "that she had
discovered him to be a foreigner only
from his speaking in a manner too Attic."
Something of this ultra-precision is perhaps to be observed to-day in the modern
Athens, be that Edinburgh or Boston.

In the ordinary speech of Englishmen
there are not a few vocables which grate
on American ears. Sometimes they are
ludicrous, sometimes they are hideous,
sometimes they seem to us simply strange.
Thus when Matthew Arnold wrote about
Tolstoï, he told us that Anna Karénina
"throws herself under the wheels of a
*goods* train." To us Americans this
sounds odd, as it is our habit to call the
means of self-destruction chosen by the
Russian heroine "a *freight* train." But
it is simply due to the accidental evolution of railroad terminology in England
and in America at the same time, whereby the same thing came to be called by a
different name on either side of the Atlantic. Neither term has a right of way
as against the other; and it would be in-

teresting to foresee which will get down to our great-grandchildren. In like manner the *keyless watch* of Great Britain is the *stem-winder* of the United States; and here, again, there is little to choose, as both words are logical.

The use of *like* for *as*, not uncommon in the Southern States, has there always been regarded as an indefensible colloquialism; but in England it is heard in the conversation of literary men of high standing, and now and again it even gets itself into print in books of good repute. It will be found, for instance, in the sketch of Macaulay which the late Cotter Morrison wrote for the series of *English Men of Letters* edited by Mr. John Morley. And Walter Bagehot represents the dwellers in old manor-houses and in rural parsonages asking, " Why can't they [the French] have Kings, Lords, and Commons, *like* we have ?" Here occasion serves to remark that Bagehot's own writing is besprinkled with Briticisms; his style is slouchy beyond belief; it is impossible to imagine a Frenchman or an American capable of thinking as clearly and as cogently as Bagehot, and willing to write as carelessly.

To be noted also is the British habit of saying "very pleased," when the tradition of the language and the best American usage alike require one to say "very much pleased." Equally noteworthy is the misuse of *without* for *unless*, condemned in America as a vulgarism, but discoverable in England in the pages of important periodical publications; for example, in the number of the *New Review* for August, 1890, we find Sir Charles Dilke, who, as a member of her Majesty's Privy Council, ought to be familiar with the Queen's English, writing that "nothing can be brought before the Vestry *without* the Vestry is duly summoned." Among the political Briticisms which deserve collection as well as political Americanisms, although far less picturesque, are to be recorded the use of *the government* when *the ministry* rather is intended, and also the habit of accepting these nouns of multitude as plural, and therefore of writing "the ministry *are*" and "the government *are*" where an American would more naturally write "the administration *is*." Another more recent Briticism is the growing habit of dropping the article, and saying that "ministers are," meaning

2

thereby that the cabinet as a whole is about to take action. As yet I have not seen " ministers is," but even this barbaric locution bids fair to be reached in course of time. It must be admitted that the terminology of politics is independent in its tendencies, and frequently " breaks the slate" of the regular grammar. It was the speech-making of an American Senator which appeared to the late George T. Lanigan as " a foretaste of that grammatical millennium when the singular verb shall lie down with the plural noun, and a little conjunction shall lead them."

Perhaps the two most frequent Briticisms and the most obvious are the use of *different to* where the American more appropriately and logically says *different from*, and the employment of *directly* and its synonym *immediately* for *as soon as* in such phrases as " *directly* he arrived, he did thus." Even Thackeray, in his most carefully written and most artistic novel, allowed Henry Esmond to write *instantly* for *as soon as*, whereby he was guilty also of an anachronism, as this blunder is a Briticism of comparatively recent origin, and is not yet to be found in the pages of any American author of authority. It is perhaps worthy of note that in that triumph of psychologic insight *Barry Lyndon*, which also is written in the first person, we find *like* for *as*, much as though it were a Hibernicism, which we do not understand it to be.

I am informed and believe—for in matters of language I prefer to testify on information and belief only, and not to make affidavit of my own knowledge, necessarily circumscribed by individual experience—I am informed and believe that an Englishman says *lift* where we say *elevator*, and that he calls that man an *agricultural laborer* whom an American would term a *farm hand*. In the one case the Briticism is the shorter, and in the other the Americanism. I am told that an Englishman calls for a *tin* of condensed milk, when an American would ask for a *can*, and that an Englishman even ventures to taste *tinned* meat, which we Americans would suspect to be tainted by the metal, although we have no prejudice against *canned* meats. I understand that an Englishman *stops* at a hotel at which an American would *stay*. I have been led to believe that an Englishwoman of fashion will go to a *swagger func-*

*tion*, at which she will expect to meet *no end* of *smart* people, meaning thereby not clever folks, but *swells*. I have heard that an Englishman speaks of a *wire*, meaning a *telegram;* and I know that an English friend of mine in New York received a letter from his sister in London, bidding him hold himself in readiness to cross the Atlantic at a day's notice, and informing him that he might " have to come over on a *wire.*" To an American, going over the ocean "on a wire" seems an unusual mode of travelling, and too Blondin-like to be attempted by less expert acrobats.

The point half-way between us and our adversary seems nearer to him; but this is an optical delusion, just as the jet of water in the centre of a fountain appears closer to the other side than to ours. So it is not easy for any one on either shore of the Atlantic to be absolutely impartial in considering the speech of those on the other. An American with a sense of the poetic cannot but prefer to the imported word *autumn* the native and more logical word *fall*, which the British have strangely suffered to drop into disuse. An American conscious of the fact that *cunning* is frequent in the mouths of his fair countrywomen, and that it is sadly wrenched from its true significance, is aware also that the British are trying to cramp our mother-tongue by limiting *bug* to a single offensive species, by giving to *bloody* an ulterior significance as of semi-profanity, and by restricting *sick* to a single form of physical wretchedness, forgetful that Peter's wife's mother once lay sick of a fever, and that an officer in her Majesty's service may even now go home on sick leave. The ordinary and broader use of *sick* is not as uncommon in England as some British critics affect to think. I have heard an Englishman defend the use of *I feel bad* for *I feel ill*, on the ground that he employed the former phrase only when he was sick enough to be above all thought of grammar.

We Americans have extended the meaning of *transom*, which, strictly speaking, was the bar across the top of a door under the fanlight itself. This American enlargement of the meaning of *transom* has not found favor at the hands of British critics, who did not protest in any way against the British restriction of the meaning of *bug*, *bloody*, and *sick.* Indeed, in the very number of the London weekly review in which we could read a protest against Mr. Howells's employment of *transom* in its more modern American meaning was to be seen an advertisement of a journalist in want of a job, and vaunting himself as expert in the writing of *leaderettes.* Surely *leaderette* is as unlovely a vocable as one could find in a Sabbath day's reading; and, moreover, it is almost unintelligible to an American, who calls that an *editorial* which the Englishman calls a *leader,* and who would term that an *editorial paragraph* which the Englishman terms a *leaderette.* Another sentence plucked from the pages of the *Saturday Review* about the same time is also almost incomprehensible to the ordinary American: " But he is so brilliant and so much by way of being complete that they will be few who read his book and do not wish to know more of him." From the context we may hazard a guess that *so much by way of being* is here synonymous with *almost.* But what would Lindley Murray say to so vile a phrase ?—that Lindley Murray whom the British invoke so often, ignoring or ignorant of the fact that he was an American. Holding with the late Richard Grant White that ours is really a grammarless tongue, and distrusting all efforts of school-masters to strait-jacket our speech into formulas borrowed from the Latin, I for one should be quite willing to abandon Lindley Murray to the British. It is not the first time that an American weed has been exhibited in England as a horticultural beauty; our common way-side mullein, for example, is cherished across the Atlantic as the " American velvet plant."

Other divergencies of usage may perhaps deserve a passing word. It is an Americanism to call him *clever* whom we deem good-natured only; and it is a Briticism to call that entertainment *smart* which we consider very fashionable; and of the two the Briticism seems the more natural outgrowth. So also the British *terminus* of Latin origin is better than the American *depot* of French origin; it is a wonder that so uncouth an absurdity as *depot* ever got into use when we had at hand the natural word *station*.

Sometimes the difference between the Americanism and Briticism is very slight. In America *coal* is put on the grate in the singular, while in England *coals* are put in the grate in the plural. In the United States *beets* are served at table as a vegetable, while in Great Britain *beet root* is served. Oddly enough, the British do not say *potato root* or *carrot root* when they order either of those esculents to be cooked, and as the American usage seems the more logical, perhaps it is more likely to prevail.

Sometimes—and indeed one might say often—a word or a usage is denounced by some British critic without due examination of the evidence on its behalf. Professor Freeman, for example, who is frequently finicky in his choice of words, objected strongly to the use of *metropolis* as descriptive of the chief city of a country, rather restricting the word to its more ecclesiastical significance as a cathedral town, and Mr. Skeat has admitted the validity of the objection. But Mr. R. O. Williams, in his recent suggestive paper on "Good English for Americans," informs us that *metropolis* was employed to indicate the most important city of the State by Macaulay, an author most careful in the use of words, and by De Quincey, a purist of the strictest sect. Nay, more, he even finds *metropolis* thus taken in the prose of Addison and in the verse of Milton.

In like manner Dr. Fitzedward Hall had no difficulty in showing that *reliable*, often objurgated as an Americanism, is to be found in a letter written in 1624 by one Richard Montagu, afterwards a bishop, and that it owes its introduction into literature to Coleridge, who used it in 1800. Dr. Hall has also shown that *scientist*, which Mr. A. J. Ellis saw fit to denounce as an "American barbaric trisyllable," was first used by an Englishman, Dr. Whewell, in 1840. One of the abiding advantages of the *New English Dictionary* of the Philological Society—an advantage which may more than counterbalance the carelessness with which its quotations have been verified—is that its columns can be used to convince even the ordinary British critic that many a word and many an expression which he is prompt to condemn as an Americanism, and therefore pestilent, is to be found in the literature of our language long before the Declaration of Independence broke the political unity of the Anglo-Saxon race. And although a negative is always difficult of proof, this same *New English Dictionary*

gives evidence in behalf of the late Mr.
White's contention that *Britisher* is not
an Americanism, but a Briticism; he said
that the word was never heard in the
mouth of an American, and, as it happens, Dr. Murray is not able to adduce in
its behalf a single quotation from any
American author.

The effort for precision, the desire to
make a word do no more than is set down
for it, the wish to have warrant for every
syllable, is neither despicable nor futile.
It is only by taking thought that language
can be bent to do our will. The sparse vocabulary and the rude idioms of the shepherd or the teamster are inadequate to
the needs of the poet and of the student.
The ideal of style is said to be the speech
of the people in the mouth of the scholar.
And Walter Bagehot, in his essay on
"Sterne and Thackeray"—one of the
few of his papers which have art and form
as well as sympathy and insight—declares
that "how language was first invented
and made we may not know, but beyond
doubt it was shaped and fashioned into
its present state by common ordinary
men and women using it for common and
ordinary purposes. They wanted a carv-

ing-knife, not a razor or lancet; and those great artists who have to use language for more exquisite purposes, who employ it to describe changing sentiments and momentary fancies, and the fluctuating and indefinite inner world, must use curious nicety and hidden but effectual artifice, else they cannot duly punctuate their thoughts and slice the fine edges of their reflections. A hair's breadth is as important to them as a yard's breadth to a common workman."

To put so sharp a point upon his style, the artist in words must choose his material with unfaltering care. He must select and store away in his scrip the best words. He must free his vocabulary from clumsy localisms, whether these be Americanisms or Briticisms. He must be true to the inherent and vital principles of our language, not yielding to temporary defections from the truth, whether these flourish in Great Britain or in the United States.

It cannot be said too often that there is no basis for the belief that somewhere there exists a sublimated English language, perfect and impeccable. This is the flawless ideal to which all artists in

style strive vainly to attain, whether they
are Englishmen or Americans, Austra-
lians or Canadians, Irish or Scotch. But
nowhere is this speech without stain
spoken by man in his daily life—not in
London, where cockneyisms abound, not
in Oxford, where university slang is lux-
uriant and where pedantry flourishes.
Nowhere has this pure and undefiled
language ever been spoken by any community. Nowhere will it ever be spoken
other than by a few men here and there
gifted by nature or trained by art. The
speech of the people in the mouth of the
scholar, that is the absolute ideal which
no man can find by travel, and which
every man must make for himself by toil,
avoiding alike the tendency of the people
towards slouching inaccuracy and the
tendency of the scholar towards academic
frigidity. Of the two, the more wholesome leaning is towards the forcible
idioms of the plain people rather than the
tamer precision of the student. The wild
flowers of speech, plucked betimes with
the dew still on them, humble and homely
and touching, such as we find in Franklin
and in Emerson, in Lowell and in Thoreau, are to be preferred infinitely before

the waxen petals of rhetoric as a school-
master arranges them.   The grammarian,
the purist, the pernicketty stickler for
trifles, is the deadly foe of good English,
rich in idioms and racy of the soil.   Every
man who has taught himself to know good
English and to love it and to delight in it,
must sympathize with Professor Lounsbury's lack of admiration "for that gram-
mar-school training which consists in
teaching the pupil how much more he
knows about our tongue than the great
masters who have moulded it, which prac-
tically sets up the claim that the only men
who are able to write English properly are
the men who have never shown any ca-
pacity to write it at all."

As to the English of the future, who
knows what the years may bring forth?
The language is alive and growing and
extending on all sides, to the grief of the
purist and the pedant, who prefer a dead
language that they can dissect at will, and
that has come to the end of its usefulness.   The existence of Briticisms and of
Americanisms and of Australianisms is a
sign of healthy vitality.   " Neither usage,"
said Professor Freeman, after contrasting
certain Americanisms and Briticisms,

"can be said to be in itself better or worse than the other. Each usage is the better in the land in which it has grown up of itself." An unprejudiced critic, if such a one could haply be found, would probably discover an equality of blemish on either side of the ocean—more precision and pedantry on the one side, and a more daring carelessness on the other. To declare a single standard of speech is impossible.

That there will ever be any broad divergence between the English language and American speech, such, for example, as differentiates the Portuguese from the Spanish, is now altogether unlikely. A divergence as wide as this has been impossible since the invention of printing, and it is even less possible since the school-master has been abroad teaching the same A B C in London, New York, Sydney, and Calcutta. Although it has ceased absolutely to be British, the chief literature of North America is still English, and must remain so, just as the chief literature of South America is still Spanish. Señor Juan Valera, declaring this truth in the preface to his delightful *Pepita Ximenez*, reminds us that "the literature of Syracuse, of Antioch, and of Alexandria was as much Greek literature as was the literature of Athens." In like manner we may recall the fact that Lucan, Seneca, Martial, and Quintilian were all of them Spaniards by birth.

That any one country shall remain or become at once the political, financial, and literary centre of the wide series of Anglo-Saxon States which now encircles the globe is almost equally unlikely. But we may be sure that that branch of our Anglo-Saxon stock will use the best English, and will perhaps see its standards of speech accepted by the other branches, which is most vigorous physically, mentally, and morally, which has the most intelligence, and which knows its duty best and does it most fearlessly.

1891

HEN the author of "The Cathedral" was accosted by the wandering Englishmen within the lofty aisles of Chartres, he cracked a joke,

" Whereat they stared, then laughed, and we were friends,
  The seas, the wars, the centuries interposed,
  Abolished in the truce of common speech
  And mutual comfort of the mother-tongue."

In this common speech other Englishmen are not always ready to acknowledge the full rights of Lowell's countryman. They would put us off with but a younger brother's portion of the mother-tongue, seeming somehow to think that they are more closely related to the common parent than we are. But Orlando, the younger son of Sir Rowland du Bois, was no villain; and though we have broken with the father-land, the mother-tongue is none the less our heritage. Indeed we

•

need not care whether the division is *per stirpes* or *per capita*, our share is not the less in either case.

Beneath the impotent protests which certain British newspapers are prone to make every now and again against the " American language " as a whole, and against the stray Americanism which has happened last to invade England, there is a tacit assumption that we Americans are outer barbarians, mere strangers, wickedly tampering with something which belongs to the British exclusively. And the outcry against the " American language " is not as shrill nor as piteous as the shriek of horror with which certain of the journals of London greet " American spelling," a hideous monster, which they feared was ready to devour them as soon as the international copyright bill should become law. In the midst of every discussion of the effect of the copyright act in Great Britain, the bugbear of " American spelling " reared its grisly head. The London *Times* declared that English publishers would never put any books into type in the United States because the people of England would never tolerate the peculiarities of

3

orthography which prevailed in American printing - offices. The *St. James's Gazette* promptly retorted that "already newspapers in London are habitually using the ugliest forms of American spelling, and those silly eccentricities do not make the slightest difference in their circulation." The *Times* and the *St. James's Gazette* might differ as to the effect of the copyright act on the profits of the printers of England, but they agreed heartily as to the total depravity of "American spelling." I think that any disinterested foreigner who might chance to hear these violent outcries would suppose that English orthography was as the law of the Medes and Persians, which altereth not ; he would be justified in believing that the system of spelling now in use in Great Britain was hallowed by the Established Church, and in some way mysteriously connected with the State religion. Indeed, no other explanation would suffice to account for the vigor, the violence, and the persistency of the protests.

Just what the British newspapers are afraid of it is not easy to say and it is difficult to declare just what they mean

when they talk of "American spelling."
Probably they do not refer to the improvements in orthography suggested by
the first great American — Benjamin
Franklin. Possibly they do refer to the
modifications in the accepted spelling
proposed by another American, Noah
Webster—not so great, and yet not to be
named slightingly by any one who knows
how fertile his labors have been for the
good of the whole country. Noah Webster, so his biographer, Mr. Scudder, tells
us, " was one of the first to carry a spirit
of democracy into letters. . . . Throughout
his work one may detect a confidence in
the common-sense of the people which
was as firm as Franklin's." But the in-
novations of Webster were hesitating and
often inconsistent; and the most of them
have been abandoned by later editors of
Webster's *American Dictionary of the
English Language.*

What, then, do British writers mean
when they animadvert upon " American
spelling?" So far as I have been able to
discover, the British journalists object to
certain minor labor-saving improvements
of American orthography, such as the
dropping of the *k* from *almanack*, the

omission of one *g* from *waggon*, and the like ; and they protest with double force, with all the strength that in them lies, against the substitution of a single *l* for a double *l* in such words as *traveller*, against the omission of the *u* from such words as *honour*, against the substitution of an *s* for a *c* in such words as *defence*, and against the transposing of the final two letters of such words as *theatre*. The objection to " American spelling" may lie deeper than I have here suggested, and it may have a wider application ; but I have done my best to state it fully and fairly as I have deduced it from a painful perusal of many columns of exacerbated British writing.

Now if I have succeeded in stating honestly the extent of the British journalistic objections to " American spelling," the unprejudiced reader may be moved to ask : " Is this all ? Are these few and slight and unimportant changes the cause of this mighty commotion ?" One may agree with Sainte - Beuve in thinking that " orthography is the beginning of literature," without discovering in these modifications from the Johnsonian canon any cause for extreme disgust. And since I have quoted Sainte-Beuve once, I venture to cite him again, and to take from the same letter of March 15, 1867, his suggestion that " if we write more correctly, let it be to express especially honest feelings and just thoughts."

Feelings may be honest though they are violent, but irritation is not the best frame of mind for just thinking. The tenacity with which some of the newspapers of London are wont to defend the accepted British orthography is perhaps due rather to feeling than to thought. Lowell told us that esthetic hatred burned nowadays with as fierce a flame as ever once theological hatred ; and any American who chances to note the force and the fervor and the frequency of the objurgations against " American spelling" in the columns of the *Saturday Review*, for example, and of the *Athenæum*, may find himself wondering as to the date of the papal bull which declared the infallibility of contemporary British orthography, and as to the place where the council of the Church was held at which it was made an article of faith.

The *Saturday Review* and the *Athenæum*, highly pitched as their voices are, yet are scarcely shriller in their cry to arms against the possible invasion of the sanctity of British orthography by "American spelling" than is the London *Times*, the solid representative of British thought, the mighty organ-voice of British feeling. Yet the *Times* is not without orthographic eccentricities of its own, as Matthew Arnold took occasion to point out. In his essay on the "Literary Influence of Academies," he asserts that "every one has noticed the way in which the *Times* chooses to spell the word *diocese;* it always spells it *diocess*, deriving it, I suppose, from *Zeus* and *census*. . . . Imagine an educated Frenchman indulging himself in an orthographical antic of this sort!"

When we read what is written in the *Times* and the *Saturday Review* and the *Athenæum*, sometimes in set articles on the subject, and even more often in casual and subsidiary slurs in the course of book-reviews, we wonder at the vehemence of the feeling displayed. If we did not know that ancient abuses are often defended with more vigor and with louder shouts than inheritances of less doubtful worth, we might suppose that

the present spelling of the English language was in a condition perfectedly satisfactory alike to scholar and to student.
Such, however, is not the case. The leading philologists of Great Britain and of
the United States have repeatedly denounced English spelling as it now is on
both sides of the Atlantic. Professor
Max Müller at Oxford is no less emphatic
than Professor Whitney at Yale. There
is now living no scholar of any repute
who any longer defends the orthodox
and ordinary orthography of the English
language.

The fact is that a little learning is quite
as dangerous a thing now as it was in
Pope's day. Those who are volubly de-
nouncing " American spelling " in the
columns of British journals are not students of the history of English speech ;
they are not scholars in English ; in so
far as they know anything of the language, they are but amateur philologists.
As a well-known writer on spelling reform once neatly remarked, " The men
who get their etymology by inspiration
are like the poor in that we have them
always with us." Although few of them
are as ignorant and dense as the unknown

unfortunate who first tortured the obviously jocular *Welsh rabbit* into a pedantic and impossible *Welsh rarebit*, still the most of their writing serves no good purpose ; to quote the apt illustration of a Western humorist, " It has as little influence as the *p* in *pneumonia*." Nor do we discover in these specimens of British journalism that abundant urbanity which etymology might lead us to look for in the writing of inhabitants of so large a city as London.

Any one who takes the trouble to inform himself on the subject will soon discover that it is only the half-educated man who defends the contemporary orthography of the English language, and who denounces the alleged " American spelling" of *center* and *honor*. The uneducated reader may wonder perchance what the *g* is doing in *sovereign ;* the half - educated reader discerns in the *g* a connecting link between the English *sovereign* and the Latin *regno ;* the well-educated reader knows that there is no philological connection whatever between *regno* and *sovereign*.

The most of those who write with ease in British journals, deploring the prevalence of " American spelling," have never carried their education so far as to acquire that foundation of wisdom which prevents a man from expressing an opinion on subjects as to which he is ignorant. The object of education, it has been said, is to make a man know what he knows, and also to know how much he does not know. Despite the close sympathy between the intellectual pursuits, a student of optics is not qualified to express an opinion in esthetics; and on the other hand, a critic of art may easily be ignorant of science. Now literature is one of the arts, and philology is a science. Though men of letters have to use words as the tools of their trade, orthography is none the less a branch of philology, and philology does not come by nature. Literature may even exist without writing, and therefore without spelling. Homer, the trouvères, and the minnesingers practised their art perhaps without the aid of letters. Writing, indeed, has no necessary connection with literature, still less has orthography. A literary critic is rarely a scientific student of language; he has no need to be; but being ignorant, it is the part of modesty for him not to expose his ignorance. To boast of it is unseemly.

Far be it from me to appear as the defender of the " American spelling " which the British journalists denounce. This " American spelling " is less absurd than the British spelling only in so far as it has varied therefrom. Even in these variations there is abundant absurdity. Once upon a time most words that now are spelled with a final *c* had an added *k*. Even now both British and American usage retains this *k* in *hammock*, although both British and Americans have dropped the needless letter from *havoc;* while the British retain the *k* at the end of *almanack* and the Americans have dropped it. Dr. Johnson was a reactionary in orthography as in politics; and in his dictionary he wilfully put a final *k* to words like *optick*, without being generally followed by the publick — as he would have spelled it. Music was then *musick*, although, even as late as Aubrey's time, it had been *musique*. In our own day we are witnessing the very gradual substitution of the logical *technic* for the form originally imported from France — *technique*. As yet, so far as I have observed, no attempts have been made to modify the foreign spelling of *clique* and *oblique*.

I am inclined to think that *technic* is replacing *technique* more rapidly — or should I say less slowly?—in the United States than in Great Britain. We Americans like to assimilate our words and to make them our own, while the British have rather a fondness for foreign phrases. A London journalist recently held up to public obloquy as an "ignorant Americanism" the word *program*, although he would have found it set down in Professor Skeat's *Etymological Dictionary*. "*Programme* was taken from the French," so a recent writer reminds us, "and in violation of analogy, seeing that, when it was imported into English, we had already *anagram, cryptogram, diogram, epigram*, etc." The logical form *program* is not common even in America, and British writers seem to prefer the French form, as British speakers still give a French pronunciation to *charade*, which in America has long since been accepted frankly as an English word. So we find Mr. Andrew Lang, in his *Angling Sketches*, referring to the *asphalte:* surely in our language the word is either *asphal-tum* or *asphalt*.

Here, if the excursus may be permitted, I should like to note also that the American willingness to acknowledge the English language as good enough for the ordinary purposes of speech shows itself in our acceptance of certain words of foreign origin as now fully naturalized, and therefore so to be treated. The Americans are inclined to consider that *formula*, for example, and *criterion* and *memorandum* and *cherub* and *bureau* are now good English words, forming their plurals by the addition of an *s*. Our first cousins, once removed, across the Atlantic seem to be still in doubt; and therefore we find them making the plurals of these words in accordance with the rules of the various languages from which the several words were derived. So in British books we meet the Latin plurals, *formulæ* and *memoranda;* the Greek plural, *criteria;* the Hebrew plural, *cherubim;* and the French plural, *bureaux.* Oddly enough, the writers who use these foreign plurals are unwilling to admit that the words thus modified is a foreign word, for more often than not they print it without italics, although frankly foreign words are carefully italicized. Possibly it is idle to look for any logic in anything which has to do with modern English orthography on either side of the ocean.

Perhaps, however, there is less even than ordinary logic in the British journalist's objection to the so-called "American spelling" of *meter ;* for why should any one insist on *metre* while unhesitatingly accepting its compound *diameter ?* Mr. John Bellows, in the preface to his inestimable French-English and English-French pocket dictionary, one of the very best books of reference ever published, informs us that "the Act of Parliament legalizing the use of the metric system in this country [England] gives the words meter, liter, gram, etc., spelled on the American plan." Perhaps now that the sanction of law has been given to this spelling, the final *er* will drive out the *re* which has usurped its place. In one of the last papers that he wrote, Lowell declared that "*center* is no Americanism ; it entered the language in that shape, and kept it at least as late as Defoe." " In the sixteenth and in the first half of the seventeenth century," says Professor

Lounsbury, "while both ways of writing these words existed side by side, the termination *er* is far more common than that in *re*. The first complete edition of Shakespeare's plays was published in 1623. In that work *sepulcher* occurs thirteen times; it is spelled eleven times with *er*. *Scepter* occurs thirty-seven times; it is not once spelled with *re*, but always with *er*. *Center* occurs twelve times, and in nine instances out of the twelve it ends in *er*." So we see that this so-called "American spelling" is fully warranted by the history of the English language. It is amusing to note how often a wider and a deeper study of English will reveal that what is suddenly denounced in Great Britain as the very latest Americanism, whether this be a variation in speech or in spelling, is shown to be really a survival of a previous usage of our language, and authorized by a host of precedents.

Of course it is idle to kick against the pricks of progress, and no doubt in due season Great Britain and her colonial dependencies will be content again to spell words that end in *er* as Shakespeare and Ben Jonson and Spenser spelled them. But when we get so far towards the orthographic millennium that we all spell *sepulcher*, the ghost of Thomas Campbell will groan within the grave at the havoc then wrought in the final line of " Hohenlinden," which will cease to end with even the outward semblance of a rhyme to the eye. We all know that

> "On Linden, when the sun was low,
> All bloodless lay the untrodden snow,
> And dark as winter was the flow
> Of Iser, rolling rapidly,"

and those of us who have persevered may remember that with one exception every fourth line of Campbell's poem ends with a *y*—the words are *rapidly, scenery, revelry, artillery, canopy,* and *chivalry*—not rhymes of surpassing distinction, any of them, but perhaps passable to a reader who will humor the final syllable. The one exception is the final line of the poem—

> " Shall be a soldier's *sepulchre*."

To no man's ear did *sepulchre* ever rhyme justly with *chivalry* and *canopy* and *artillery*, although Campbell may have so contorted his vision that he evoked the dim spook of a rhyme in his mind's eye.

A rhyme to the eye is a sorry thing at best, and it is sorriest when it depends on an inaccurate and evanescent orthography.

Dr. Johnson was as illogical in his keeping in and leaving out of the *u* in words like *honor* and *governor* as he was in many other things; and the makers of later dictionaries have departed widely from his practice, those in Great Britain still halting half-way, while those in the United States have gone on to the bitter end. The illogic of the great lexicographer is shown in his omission of the *u* from *exterior* and *posterior*, and his retention of it in the kindred words *interiour* and *anteriour;* this, indeed, seems like wilful perversity, and justifies Hood's merry jest about " Dr. Johnson's Contradictionary." The half-way measures of later British lexicographers are shown in their omission of the *u* from words which Dr. Johnson spelled *emperour, governour, oratour, horrour,* and *dolour,* while still retaining it in *favour* and *honour* and a few others.

The reason for his disgust generally given by the London man of letters who is annoyed by the " American spelling" of *honor* and *favor* is that these words are not derived directly from the Latin, but indirectly through the French; this is the plea put forward by the late Archbishop Trench. Even if this plea were pertinent, the application of this theory is not consistent in current British orthography, which prescribes the omission of the *u* from *error* and *emperor*, and its retention in *colour* and *honour*—although all four words are alike derived from the Latin through the French. And this plea fails absolutely to account for the *u* which the British insist on preserving in *harbour* and in *neighbour*, words not derived from the Latin at all, whether directly or indirectly through the French. An American may well ask, " If the *u* in *honour* teaches etymology, what does the *u* in *harbour* teach?" There is no doubt that the *u* in *harbour* teaches a false etymology; and there is no doubt also that the *u* in *honour* has been made to teach a false etymology, for Trench's derivation of this final *our* from the French *eur* is absurd, as the old French was *our*, and sometimes *ur*, sometimes even *or*. Pseudophilology of this sort is no new thing. Professor Max Müller tells us that the Roman prigs used to spell *cena* (to show

4

their knowledge of Greek), *coena*, as if the word were somehow connected with κοινή.

Thus we see that the *u* in *honour* suggests a false etymology; so does the *ue* in *tongue*, and the *g* in *sovereign*, and the *c* in *scent*, and the *s* in *island*, and the *mp* in *comptroller*, and the *h* in *rhyme;* and there are many more of our ordinary orthographies which are quite as misleading from a philological point of view. As Professor Hadley mildly put it, " our common spelling is often an untrustworthy guide to etymology." But why should we expect or desire spelling to be a guide to etymology? If it is to be a guide at all, we may fairly insist on its being trustworthy, and so we cannot help thinking scorn of those who insist on retaining a superfluous *u* in *honour*.

But why should orthography be made subservient to etymology? What have the two things in common? They exist for wholly different ends, to be attained by wholly different means. To bend either from its own work to the aid of the other is to impair the utility of both. This truth is recognized by all etymologists, and by all students of language, although it has not yet found acceptance among men of letters, who are rarely students of language in the scientific sense. "It may be observed," Mr. Sweet declares, "that it is mainly among the class of half-taught dabblers in philology that etymological spelling has found its supporters;" and he goes on to say that "all true philologists and philological bodies have uniformly denounced it as a monstrous absurdity both from a practical and a scientific point of view." I should never dare to apply to the late Archbishop Trench and the London journalists who echo his errors so harsh a phrase as Mr. Sweet's "half-taught dabblers in philology;" but when a fellow-Englishman uses it perhaps I may venture to quote it without reproach.

As I have said before, the alleged "American spelling" differs but very slightly from that which prevails in England. A wandering New-Yorker who rambles through London is able to collect now and again evidences of orthographic survivals which give him a sudden sense of being in an older country than his own. I have seen a man whose home was near Gramercy Park stop short

in the middle of a little street in Mayfair,
and point with ecstatic delight to the strip
of paper across the glass door of a bar pro-
claiming that *CYDER* was sold within.
I have seen the same man thrill with pure
joy before the shop of a *chymist* in the
window of which *corn-plaisters* were offered for sale. And this same New-Yorker was carried back across the years when
he noted the extra *g* in the British *waggon*—an orthographic fifth wheel, if ever
there was one; he smiled at the *k* which
lingers at the end of the British *almanack;* he wondered why a British house
should have *storeys* when an American
house has *stories;* and he disliked intensely the wanton *e* wherewith British
printers have recently disfigured *form*
which in the latest London typographi-
cal vocabularies appears as *forme*. This
*e* in *form* is a gratuitous addition, and
therefore contrary to the trend of spelling reform, which aims at the suppression
of all arbitrary and needless letters. Most
of the American modifications of the
Johnsonian orthography have been labor-
saving devices, like the dropping of *u* in
*color* and of one *l* in *traveler*, in an effort
at simplification, and in accord with the

irresistible tendency of mankind to cut
across lots.

The so-called "American spelling" differs from the spelling which obtains in
England only in so far as it has yielded
a little more readily to the forces which
make for progress, for uniformity, for
logic, for common-sense. But just how
fortuitous and chaotic the condition of
English spelling is nowadays both in
Great Britain and in the United States
no man knows who has not taken the
trouble to investigate for himself. In
England, the reactionary orthography of
Samuel Johnson is no longer accepted by
all. In America, the revolutionary orthography of Noah Webster has been re-
ceded from even by his own inheritors.
There is no standard, no authority, not
even that of a powerful, resolute, and
domineering personality.

Perhaps the attitude of philologists
towards the present spelling of the English language, and their opinion of those
who are up in arms in defence of it, have
never been more tersely stated than in
Professor Lounsbury's recent and most
admirable *Studies in Chaucer*, a work
which I should term eminently scholarly,

if that phrase did not perhaps give a false impression of a book wherein the results of learning are set forth with the most adroit literary art, and with an uninsistent but omnipresent humor, which is a constant delight to the reader :

" There is certainly nothing more contemptible than our present spelling, unless it be the reasons usually given for clinging to it. The divorce which has unfortunately almost always existed between English letters and English scholarship makes nowhere a more pointed exhibition of itself than in the comments which men of real literary ability make upon proposals to change or modify the cast-iron framework in which our words are now clothed. On one side there is an absolute agreement of view on the part of those who are authorized by their knowledge of the subject to pronounce an opinion. These are well aware that the present orthography hides the history of the word instead of revealing it ; that it is a stumbling-block in the way of derivation or of pronunciation instead of a guide to it; that it is not in any sense a growth or development, but a mechanical malformation, which owes its existence to the

ignorance of early printers and the necessity of consulting the convenience of
printing-offices. This consensus of scholars makes the slightest possible impression upon men of letters throughout the
whole great Anglo-Saxon community.
There is hardly one of them who is not
calmly confident of the superiority of his
opinion to that of the most famous special students who have spent years in ex-
amining the subject. There is hardly one
of them who does not fancy he is manifest-
ing a noble conservatism by holding fast
to some spelling peculiarly absurd, and
thereby maintaining a bulwark against
the ruin of the tongue. There is hardly
one of them who has any hesitation in discussing the question in its entirety, while
every word he utters shows that he does
not even understand its elementary principles. There would be something thor-
oughly comic in turning into a fierce international dispute the question of spelling
*honor* without the *u*, were it not for the
depression which every student of the language cannot well help feeling in contem-
plating the hopeless abysmal ignorance
of the history of the tongue which any
educated man must first possess in order

to become excited over the subject at all."
(*Studies in Chaucer*, vol. iii., pp. 265–7.)

Pronunciation is slowly but steadily changing. Sometimes it is going further and further away from the orthography; for example, *either* and *neither* are getting more and more to have in their first syllable the long *i* sound instead of the long *e* sound which they had once. Sometimes it is being modified to agree with the orthography; for example, the older pronunciations of *again* to rhyme with *men*, and of *been* to rhyme with *pin*, in which I was carefully trained as a boy, seem to me to be giving way before a pronunciation in exact accord with the spelling, *again* to rhyme with *pain*, and *been* to rhyme with *seen*. These two illustrations are from the necessarily circumscribed experience of a single observer, and the observation of others may not bear me out in my opinion; but though the illustrations fall to the ground, the main assertion, that pronunciation is changing, is indisputable.

No doubt the change is less rapid than it was before the invention of printing; far less rapid than it was before the days of the public-school and of the morning

newspaper. There are variations of pronunciation in different parts of the United
States and of Great Britain as there are
variations of vocabulary; but in the future there will be a constantly increasing
tendency for these variations to disappear. There are irresistible forces making
for uniformity — forces which are crush-
ing out Platt-Deutsch in Germany, Pro-
vençal in France, Romansch in Switzer-
land. There is a desire to see a standard
set up to which all may strive to conform.
In France a standard of pronunciation is
found at the performances of the Comédie
Française; and in Germany, what is almost a standard of vocabulary has been
set in what is now known as *Bühne-
Deutsch*.

In France the Academy was constitu-
ted chiefly to be a guardian of the language; and the Academy, properly con-
servative as it needs must be, is engaged
in a slow reform of French orthography,
yielding to the popular demand deco-
rously and judiciously. By official action,
also, the orthography of German has been
simplified and made more logical and
brought into closer relation with modern
pronunciation. Even more thorough re-

forms have been carried through in Italy, in Spain, and in Holland. Yet neither French nor German, not Italian, Spanish, or Dutch, stood half as much in need of the broom of reform as English, for in no one of these languages were there so many dark corners which needed cleaning out; in no one of them the difference between orthography and pronunciation as wide ; and in no one of them was the accepted spelling debased by numberless false etymologies. Sometimes it seems as though our orthography is altogether vile; that it is most intolerable and not to be endured; that it calls not for the broom of reform, but rather for the besom of destruction.

For any elaborate and far-reaching scheme of spelling reform, seemingly, the time has not yet come, although, for all we know, we may be approaching it all unwittingly, as few of us in 1860 foresaw the Emancipation Proclamation of 1863. In the mean while, what is needed on both sides of the Atlantic, in the United States as well as in Great Britain, is a conviction that the existing orthography of English is not sacred, and that to tamper with it is not high-treason. What is needed is the consciousness that neither Samuel Johnson nor Noah Webster compiled his dictionary under direct inspiration. What is needed is an awakening to the fact that our spelling, so far from being immaculate at its best, is, at its best, hardly less absurd than the hap-hazard, rule-of-thumb, funnily phonetic spelling of Artemus Ward and of Josh Billings. What is needed is anything which will break up the lethargy of satisfaction with the accepted orthography, and help to open the eyes of readers and writers to the stupidity of the present system and tend to make them discontented with it.

So the few and slight divergences between the orthography obtaining in Great Britain and the orthography obtaining in the United States are not to be deplored. The *cyder* on the door of the London barroom and the *catalog* in the pages of the New York *Library Journal* both subserve the useful purpose of making people alive to the possibilities of an amended orthography. Thus the so-called "American spelling" helps along a good cause—and so, also, do the British assaults upon it.

1892

# THE LITERARY INDEPENDENCE
## OF THE UNITED STATES

N the evening of the Tuesday following the first Monday of next November, after the citizens of the several States shall have cast their ballots for the candidates of their choice, the boys of New York, in accord with their immemorial custom on election night, will illuminate the streets of the city with countless bonfires, not knowing, any of them, that they are thus commemorating Guy Faux and the discovery of the Gunpowder Plot. And yet such is the fact, as Doctor Eggleston has ascertained beyond all question. What British boys are pleased to remember on the 5th of November, American boys have forgotten, although they keep alive the memorial fires on the evening of the Tuesday following the first Monday in November, be that the 5th or not, as the almanac may declare. In like manner the "dressing up as a Guy" still survives also in New York, in the parades of the "fantasticals" on Thanksgiving Day — the last Thursday in November. So hard is it for old customs to die out. Perhaps the British 5th of November was in its turn a survival of some pagan rite ignorantly lingering as late as the Gunpowder Plot, and thereafter identified with the fate of Guy Faux.

We cannot help being the descendants of our ancestors; and no tariff, however high and however complicated by *ad valorem* duties, can keep out of these United States the traditions, the beliefs, the habits, the feelings of the immigrants whose children we are. That those who have left a great country, England or France or Germany, should look back to that country as the centre of light, is natural—perhaps it is inevitable. But that their children should continue to do so, natural enough for a while, is not inevitable. Even though the colonist succeeds in breaking the political tie which binds him to the country whence his fathers came, there is no real independence unless he lays aside also the habit of intellectual deference; and that is as arduous, as difficult, and as long a task as any one ever undertook. None the less is it absolutely necessary if a people is to speak with its own voice and not with borrowed tongues—if its independence is to be complete and final.

In Mr. Henry Cabot Lodge's interesting and stimulant volume called *Studies in History* there is no essay more interesting or more stimulating than that on " Colonialism in the United States." In two-score pages Mr. Lodge distinguishes colonialism from provincialism, with which it is sometimes confounded, and then shows how the thirteen United States, having once been colonies, still breathed the colonial spirit long after their political independence was fully established. He recalls the fact that one half of the people disliked Washington's proclamation of neutrality as between France and Great Britain, because it seemed " hostile to France," while the other approved of it for the same reason. We Americans at the beginning of this century were still engaged in fighting over again all the battles of Europe.

But Washington was an American, not a European, and so was Hamilton; and they kept us true to the line of our national development.

Even before the Revolution, when "the travelled American, the *petit-maître* of the colonies," so Hawthorne reminds us, was "the ape of London foppery, as the newspaper was the semblance of the London journals"—even then there were Americans, like Franklin, for example, who had nothing of the colonist about them, who were at once cosmopolitan and American. Mr. Lodge is right in calling Franklin's *Autobiography* "the corner-stone, the first great work of American literature."

After the War of 1812 the politics of the United States ceased to depend in any way on the politics of Europe; and our elections began to turn solely on questions of domestic policy. So our commerce and our manufactures freed themselves from reliance on England or France. An unending succession of inventions showed the ingenuity of the American. In law, the autonomy of the separate States permitted a variety of juristic experiment, the best results of which have been copied now in the legislature of Great Britain. " But the colonial spirit "—to quote Mr. Lodge again —" cast out from our politics and fast disappearing from business and the professions, still clung closely to literature, which must always be the best and last expression of a national mode of thought."

The colonial attitude in literature was unwittingly encouraged by Congress, which, by refusing to pass an international copyright bill, and thus secure to the British author the control of his own works, permitted the foreigner to be plundered, and forced the native author to sell his wares in competition with stolen goods. Sir Henry Sumner Maine declared—in his work on *Popular Government* (p. 247) — that the neglect to give copyright to foreign "writers has condemned the whole American community to a literary servitude unparalleled in the history of thought." This, of course, is the violent over-statement of an enemy; but there was a percentage of truth in it once. To show just what the American literary attitude was in the early years of this century, Mr. Lodge instances Coop-

er's first novel, *Precaution*, now wholly
forgotten, and fortunately, for its characters, its scenery, "its conventional phrases
were all English; worst and most extraordinary of all, it professed to be by
an English author, and was received on
that theory without suspicion." And
Mr. Lodge tersely sums up the situation by saying that "the first step of an
American entering upon a literary career
was to pretend to be an Englishman in
order that he might win the approval,
not of Englishmen, but of his own countrymen."

Cooper was too good an American to
be content with the cast-off garments of
British novelists; and in 1821, a year after the appearance of *Precaution*, he published *The Spy*, and never thereafter was
there any need for an American novelist
to masquerade as an Englishman. Yet
his fellow-countrymen thought to compliment Cooper by calling him "the American Scott." And more than a quarter
of a century later, when Lowell put forth
his *Fable for Critics* there was abundant
colonialism in our literature, if we may
accept the satirist's picture of the mass-
meeting of

"The American Bulwers, Disraelis, and Scotts.

. . . . . . .

By the way, 'tis a fact that displays what profusions
Of all kinds of greatness bless free institutions,
That while the Old World has produced barely eight
Of such poets as all men agree to call great,
And of other great characters nearly a score —
One might safely say less than that rather than more—
With you every year a whole crop is begotten,
They're as much of a staple as corn is or cotton;
Why, there's scarcely a huddle of log-huts and shanties
That has not brought forth its own Miltons and
    Dantes;                                              \
I myself know ten Byrons, one Coleridge, three
    Shelleys,
Two Raphaels, six Titians (I think), one Apelles,
Leonardos and Rubenses plenty as lichens,
One (but that one is plenty) American Dickens,
A whole flock of Lambs, any number of Tennysons—
In short, if a man has the luck to have any sons,
He may feel pretty certain that one out of twain
Will be some very great person over again."

After Cooper came Hawthorne and
Poe, intensely American, both of them,
although in different fashion. In due
season Mrs. Stowe brought out one book
which set forth fearlessly a situation un-
deniably (and most unfortunately) American. Then came the war, which stiffened
our national consciousness, and by giving
us something to be proud of, killed the
earlier habit of brag. Among later story-
tellers who study American life as it is,

and without any taint of Briticism, are
the author of *The Adventures of Huckleberry Finn*, the author of *The Rise of Silas Lapham*, the author of *The Hoosier
Schoolmaster*, and the author of *Old Creole
Days*, all aggressively American, all devoid of the slightest suggestion of colonialism, all possessing a wholesome mistrust
of British traditions, British standards,
and British methods. Some of his fellow-
countrymen and contemporaries complained that Cooper was not proud of
being called "the American Scott;" and
if we want to see how far we have travelled away from colonialism of this sort
we have only to imagine the laughter
with which Mark Twain would greet any
critic who thought to compliment him
by calling him the American Burnand!

That this is an enormous gain is obvious enough. American authors are now
writing for their fellow-countrymen and
about their fellow-countrymen. If, as
Matthew Arnold declared, "the end and
aim of all literature is, if one considers it
attentively, nothing but that—a criticism
of life," then the literature likely to be
most useful, most invigorating, and most
satisfactory to Americans should be a

criticism of life in America. Whether
or not the spirit of colonialism still survives in these United States sufficiently
to make the majority of readers here prefer books of British authorship is a question hardly worth asking, it seems to me,
although there are some, both in London
and in New York, who would answer it
in the affirmative. To those of us who
happened to be in London during the
closing days of our long struggle for the
Copyright act of 1891 it was obvious that
many British authors believed that un-
bounded affluence was about to burst
upon them. They accepted Sir Henry
Maine's view as to the literary poverty
of America, and apparently did not know
that there were American authors standing ready to supply the American demand as soon as they should be relieved
from an enforced competition with stolen
goods.

These British authors thought that the
passage of the act opened a boundless
field for them to enter in and take possession of; and no doubt some of the
American opponents of the bill were of
the same opinion. Of course we all see
now, what some of us who had studied

the conditions of the book-trade foresaw, that the instant result of the Copyright act must needs be a decrease in the number of books of British authorship sold in the United States. As soon as there was only one authorized publisher engaged in pushing a British book in America, in the place of a dozen unauthorized publishers forced to a frantic and cutthroat competition, the British book had to sell on its merits alone, without the aid of any premium of cheapness. As soon as all books had to be paid for by the publisher, the book of native authorship had its natural preference; and now the inferior and doubtful books of foreign authorship are ceasing to be reprinted here. This is a tendency which will increase with time, and very properly, since every nation ought to be able to supply its own second-rate books, and to borrow from abroad only the best that the foreigner has to offer it. And it cannot be said too often or too emphatically that the British are foreigners, and that their ideals in life, in literature, in politics, in taste, in art, are not our ideals.

The decrease in the proportion of British books published in America, sharply accelerated, no doubt, by the Copyright act of 1891, has been going on ever since Cooper published *The Spy*, now more than threescore years and ten ago. It occurred to me that it would be useful to show exactly the rate at which the American book had been gaining upon the British book, and to discover whether the native author had overtaken the foreigner or was likely to do so. To this end I have considered the books issued during the past thirty years by two of the leading publishing houses of America: Messrs. Harper & Brothers, and Messrs. Houghton, Mifflin & Company. Messrs. Harper & Brothers have always maintained very close relations with the leading authors of Great Britain; and to them, far more than to any one other American publishing house, have the most popular writers of England intrusted the American editions of their works. Messrs. Houghton, Mifflin & Company, on the other hand, succeeding to the firms of Ticknor & Fields, and of Fields, Osgood & Company, have always devoted themselves more especially to books of American authorship. These two great houses represent different traditions, and it seemed to me therefore that a comparison of their present catalogues with their catalogues of thirty years ago would not be without profit. I have to thank both these firms for their kindly assistance, without which it would have been impossible for me to prepare the present paper.

I have been furnished with a list of the books published by Messrs. Harper & Brothers in the years 1861, 1871, 1881, and 1891; and I propose to show how the book of American authorship has gained on the book of British authorship in three decades. From all the lists I begin by discarding the classic authors of our language. There was scarcely any American literature before Cooper's *Spy*, and of course all the glorious roll of English authors who wrote before 1776 are as much a part of our having as the common law itself. For kindred reasons I throw out all new editions and all text-books and all school-books.

Making these deductions (and they naturally decrease very much the apparent number of books published during any one year), we find that in the year 1861 Messrs. Harper & Brothers issued twenty-four books, of which fourteen were of British authorship (including George Eliot's *Silas Marner*) and seven of American authorship (including Motley's *United Netherlands* and Mr. Curtis's *Trumps*) ; three books sent forth by them were translated from foreign languages.

In 1871 Messrs Harper & Brothers published fifty-seven books, and of these thirty - six were of British authorship, twenty were by American writers, and one was a translation.

In 1881 they sent forth ninety - eight books, of which sixty-six were by British authors (including some forty-seven numbers of the Franklin Square Library) and twenty - six were by American authors, while six were translations from foreign languages. It is to be noted that in 1881 we were in the very thick of piracy, and that Messrs. Harper & Brothers were engaged in pushing vigorously the Franklin Square Library, which they had devised as a weapon to fight the reprinters with.

In 1891 the Copyright act became operative on the 1st of July. During that year Messrs. Harper & Brothers issued seventy-six books, of which twenty-seven were of British authorship and forty-one

of American, while eight were translations.   It is to be noted here that the
translations of 1891 were nearly all made
in America, while those of 1861 and of
1881 were the work of British writers.
In the books of British authorship are in-
cluded all those issued only in paper cov-
ers in the new Franklin Square Library.
Of course, Messrs. Harper & Brothers issued every year many more books than I
have counted ; but I have, as I said, omitted all new editions, all school-books, and
all reprints of the classics of our own or
any other language, as not falling within
the scope of this inquiry.   To decide exactly what to include or to exclude was
not always easy, but I have tried to be
consistent, and I believe that the figures
here given are fairly accurate.   They
show that a house which published in
1861 twice as many books of British
authorship as of American, published in
1891 one-third more books of American
authorship than of British.   They show
also that the actual number of American
books issued by this firm increased with
every decade, and was in 1891 almost six
times as large as it was thirty years before.

The present house of Houghton, Mifflin & Company is descended on one side from the firm of Hurd & Houghton, and on the other from the firm which was successively William D. Ticknor & Company, Ticknor & Fields, Fields, Osgood & Company, and James R. Osgood & Company. I am sorry to say that I have not been able to get a complete catalogue of the books published by Ticknor & Fields in 1861, but I have found certain lists of books published by them about that time: one of these lists contains four American books, three British, and one translation from a foreign tongue; in another there are ten books of British authorship and ten of American; and in a third there are six British authors represented and eight American.

In 1871 the firm was James R. Osgood & Company, and the proportion of books of American authorship was steadily increasing. I have not been able to find a full and complete list, but I know that the house published that year at least twenty-eight books by American authors, ten by British writers, and three translated from a modern language.

In 1881 the firm had become Hough-

ton, Mifflin & Company, and it has kindly provided me with an accurate list
of its publications during these twelve
months. Omitting, as before, all new editions, we find that the house issued that
year thirty - eight books by Americans,
seven by British authors, and eleven volumes of translations.

In 1891 the proportion of native works
still further increased. The American
books published in that year by Messrs.
Houghton, Mifflin & Company were six-
ty-nine, while the firm issued only seven
volumes by British authors and two translations. A comparison of these figures
with those of thirty years before show
that the predecessors of Messrs. Houghton, Mifflin & Company published in 1861
about as many books of British authorship as of American; while in 1891 the
firm sent forth ten times as many American books as it did British.

In going over the lists of Messrs. Harper & Brothers and of Messrs. Houghton,
Mifflin & Company, I have resolutely cast
out of account all school-books, because
a consideration of these might have giv-
en a false impression, since the school-
books of all Americans who were boys

in 1861 were already of American authorship. I was a boy myself in 1861, and I
never saw a school-book of British origin
until after I had been in college for a
year or two, and then it was only a single manual of political economy. When
Noah Webster issued, in 1783, the first
part of a *Grammatical Institute of the
English Language*, afterwards known as
*Webster's Spelling Book*, and as such sold
for half a century to the extent of a
million copies a year, an example was set
which other American educators were
prompt to follow.

For nearly a hundred years now the
American school-boy has been supplied
with American books suited to American conditions and inculcating American
ideas. Nor is there any likelihood that
this fortunate condition will ever change.
The American Book Company, a publishing firm formed by the consolidation
of four or five of the leading school-book
houses of this country, supplies probably
four-fifths of the books used in American
schools. I have recently made a careful
examination of its complete classified
price-list of school and college text-
books, with the eminently satisfactory

result of finding in the first 500 titles only one book of foreign authorship.

Perhaps it was in consequence of the wholesome Americanism imparted in the school-room that American boys and girls demanded other books of American authorship. Certain it was that the department of the publishing trade which handles "juveniles," as they are called, gave an early preference to books describing life in America or from an American point of view. Peter Parley was a pioneer, and Jacob Abbott followed after; and I confess I am sorry for the boys and girls of Great Britain who did not know the joy of travelling through Europe with Rollo and Uncle George, the omniscient. From my own childhood I can recall only one volume of British origin, although of American manufacture; it was a sturdy tome called *The Boy's Own Book*, and it had strange wood-cuts of strangely chubby youths in strange Eton jackets.

In Doctor Holmes's paper on "The Seasons" (to be found in *Pages from an Old Volume of Life*), it is made evident that the American children of the second decade of this century were less fortunate than those of the seventh decade. Doc-

tor Holmes tells us that he was educated
on Miss Edgeworth and *Evenings at Home.*
"There we found ourselves in a strange
world, where James was called Jem, not
Jim, as we always heard it; where one
found cowslips in the fields, while what
we saw were buttercups; where naughty
school-boys got through a gap in the
hedge to steal Farmer Giles's red-streaks,
instead of shinning over the fence to hook
old Daddy Jones's Baldwins; where there
were larks and nightingales instead of
yellow-birds and bobolinks; where the
robin was a little domestic bird that fed
at the table, instead of a great, fidgety,
jerky, whooping thrush; where poor people lived in thatched cottages, instead of
shingled ten-footers; where the tables
were made of deal; where every village
had its parson and clerk and beadle, its
green-grocer, its apothecary who visited
the sick, and its bar-maid who served out
ale" (pp. 172–3).

And with the witty wisdom which is
the secret of the Autocrat's power over
us, he continues: "What a mess—there
is no other word for it—what a mess was
made of it in our young minds in the attempt to reconcile what we read about

with what we saw ! It was like putting a picture of Regent's Park in one side of a stereoscope and a picture of Boston Common on the other, and trying to make one of them. The end was that we all grew up with a mental squint which we could never get rid of. We saw the lark and the cowslip and the rest on the printed page with one eye, the bobolink and the buttercup, and so on, with the other in nature. This world is always a riddle to us at best; but those English children's books seemed so perfectly simple and natural, and yet were so alien to our youthful experiences that the Houyhnhnm primer could not have muddled our intellects more hopelessly."

The colonial habit of dependence on England for literature and of deference to British opinion is to be seen in the history of the American drama quite as distinctly as in the other departments of literature, and it is not yet wholly extinct. At first, of course, all our actors were of British birth. When the first American comedy, Royall Tyler's "Contrast," was played at the John Street Theatre in New York in 1787, the character of Jonathan the Yankee was undertaken by Thomas

Wignell, a native of England. Thomas
Abthorpe Cooper was criticised in London as an American, but he had been
born in Great Britain. Edwin Forrest
was the first distinguished tragedian who
was a native of our continent. Since he
set the example many an American actor
has appeared in England, and Mr. Au-
gustin Daly has taken his whole company of comedians to Europe repeatedly.
Nowadays there are always performers of American birth and training in
half a dozen of the leading London theatres.

Indeed, it might fairly be said that acting was the first of the arts to develop
here in America; beyond all question it
was the first that we began to export.
But the art of the native American dramatist long lagged behind that of the native
American actor. Perhaps even now there
is still a lingering survival of the prejudice in favor of foreign plays, or, at least,
against plays of American authorship.
At present the foreign play most likely
to be in favor is the French, but when
the theatre was young in this country our
sole reliance was on the British stage.
Now we get light from Berlin and from

Paris; then we saw no ray of hope except from London.

So complete was the dependence of the
Park Theatre on Drury Lane and on Co-
vent Garden in the early part of this century, that when our first native dramatist,
William Dunlap, made adaptations of
Kotzebue's plays he took good care not
to avow his share in the work, allowing
it to be supposed that his versions of the
German originals were those which had
been made for the London stage. Even
as late as 1812, when Mr. J. N. Barker
dramatized *Marmion* " the prejudice then
existing against American authors"—to
quote the words of Mr. Ireland, the his-
torian of the New York stage—" was so
great that the play was announced as the
production of an English dramatist, and
thus, with its fine cast, commanded an
extraordinary success." Perhaps this is
even more pitiful than Cooper's pretend-
ing to be an Englishman in his first novel.

To show the changes which have taken
place in the composition of our play-bills
during the past thirty years, I have had
lists made of the plays which were adver-
tised for performance in the first full
week of January in 1861, 1871, 1881, and

1891. The result of the consideration of these lists is not as convincing as one could wish, for the performances of a single week are scarcely enough to furnish matter for the adequate comparison of one year with another. Yet the comparison is not without interest, and it seems to me indisputably instructive. All grand operas, all circuses, all menageries, all dime museums, all negro minstrel entertainments, and all those strange performances known, for some inscrutable reason, as "variety shows," are here left out of court, as having little or no connection with literature.

Making these deductions, we find that there were open in New York in the first week of January, 1861, seven places of amusement devoted to the drama, at only two of which were the plays wholly of American authorship; although at a third, where Edwin Forrest was acting, the American tragedy of "The Gladiator" shared the bill with the British tragedy of "Damon and Pythias." At the rest of the theatres the plays were of British authorship, that at Wallack's being "Pauline," a British dramatization of a French novel.

In the corresponding week of 1871 after making the same omissions, and after deducting also the performances in foreign languages, always very frequent in a city with a population as cosmopolitan as ours—making these allowances, we find seven theatres, at which three British plays are being performed and three American plays, and one play, if it can so be called, " The Black Crook," which was an American adaptation from the German. There was at this time a temporary prevalence of negro minstrelsy and the variety show.

In 1881 the New Yorker who went to the theatre during the first week in January had his choice of fifteen performances, and he could see nine plays of American authorship, two American adaptations from the German, two British adaptations from the French, and two plays of British authorship. The proportion of American plays seems overwhelming, and it was probably not maintained throughout the year, although the preceding decade had seen an extraordinary development of the American drama. Among those to be seen at this time in New York were " The Danites,"

"Hazel Kirke," and "The Banker's Daughter."

When we come to 1891 we see that the list of theatres offering a dramatic entertainment in the English language has swollen to twenty-one, and we note that the variety shows and the negro minstrel performances are now infrequent. At these twenty-one theatres we could see thirteen plays of American authorship, besides two American adaptations from the German, while at the same time there were also visible five plays by British authors and one British adaptation from the French. I may add also, and of my own knowledge, that the plays which were most popular, and therefore most profitable at this time, were all to be found among the thirteen of American authorship. It is a fact also that for fully forty years now the great pecuniary successes of the American theatre have been gained by plays of American life, and more especially of American character. "Uncle Tom's Cabin," "Rip Van Winkle," "Colonel Sellers," "My Partner," "The Danites," "The Banker's Daughter," "Held by the Enemy," and "Shenandoah" have had no foreign rivals in popularity except "The

Two Orphans." Possibly exception should also be made of " The Shaughraun" and " Hazel Kirke," both written in America, although dealing with life in Europe.

It is to be noted that the Copyright act of 1891 has had, and will have, but little effect upon the foreign dramatist, because, for twenty years and more, judicial decisions in the United States courts had accorded him a full protection for his stage-right under the common law. Thus the American dramatist had been freed from the necessity of vending his wares in competition with stolen goods long before a like privilege had been vouchsafed to the American novelist.

A careful study of the figures here presented will convince the disinterested critic that the American dramatist has passed his foreign rival in the race for popularity, just as a careful study of the successive lists of Messrs. Harper & Brothers and Messrs. Houghton, Mifflin & Company will prove that the American author has also overtaken the foreigner. If there was truth once in Sir Henry Sumner Maine's assertion that we Americans offered the example of a literary servitude without parallel, that assertion is true no longer. The American author is now conscious of a demand from the American public for plays and for books which reflect American life and embody American character. Before another decade has closed the century, the proportion of works of foreign authorship to be seen in our book-stores and in our theatres is certain to be smaller still. Sooner or later the time will come when it will be profitable to reproduce in America only the best of books of foreign authors and only the best plays of foreign dramatists.

At the same time that the American author has been taking possession of his own country he has also been conquering abroad. I have not had time for the needful and laborious calculation, but I believe that an examination of the files of the London *Athenæum* and *Saturday Review* of 1861 would show that very few books of American authorship were deemed worthy of reprint and review in England, while an examination of their files for 1891 would reveal a surprisingly large proportion of books of American origin now considered as entitled to criticism. And I believe that this proportion is steadily increasing, and that more and more books

published in the United States are every
year reprinted in Great Britain, or exported for sale in London in editions of
satisfactory size.

Of course the reputation of American
authors has been spread abroad in England largely by the agency of the great
American illustrated magazines, which
have now an enormous circulation on the
other side of the Atlantic. There are at
least two American magazines which far
outsell in England itself any British magazine of corresponding pretensions. A
few British magazines and reviews continue to be imported into the United
States, but they are very few indeed; I
think that the total number of copies imported is less than the number exported
of either of the two great American illustrated monthlies.

It is pleasant to be able to assert that
this wide-spread popularity of the American magazines in England has not been
due to any attempt to cater to the English
market. On the contrary, the more obviously and frankly American these magazines are, the more marked is their success in England. No doubt a large part
of this popularity is due to American

superiority in wood-engraving, in process work, in printing, and to the liber-
ality of the American publisher in paying
for these embellishments; but a share as
large is due to the skill with which the
American magazines are edited, to their
freshness, their brightness, their vivacity,
to their national flavor, and especially to
their larger scope and to their stronger
understanding of the capabilities and the
opportunities of the modern periodical.

1892

# THE CENTENARY OF FENIMORE COOPER

OST appropriate is it that the first literary centenary which we were called upon to commemorate one hundred years after the adoption of the Constitution that knit these States into a nation should be the birthday of the author who has done the most to make us known to the nations of Europe. In the first year of Washington's first term as President, on the fifteenth day of September, 1789, was born James Fenimore Cooper, the first of American novelists, and the first American author to carry our flag outside the limits of our language. Franklin was the earliest American who had fame among foreigners; but his wide popularity was due rather to his achievements as a philosopher, as a physicist, as a statesman, than to his labors as an author. Irving was six years older than Cooper, and his reputation was as high in England as at home; yet to this day he is little more than a name to those who do not speak our mother-tongue. But after Cooper had published *The Spy*, *The Last of the Mohicans*, and *The Pilot* his popularity was cosmopolitan; he was almost as widely read in France, in Germany, and in Italy as in Great Britain and the United States. Only one American book has ever since attained the international success of these of Cooper's— *Uncle Tom's Cabin*, and only one American author has since gained a name at all commensurate with Cooper's abroad— Poe. Here in these United States we know what Emerson was to us and what he did for us and what our debt is to him; but the French and the Germans and the Italians do not know Emerson. When Professor Boyesen visited Hugo some ten years ago he found that the great French lyrist had never heard of Emerson. I have a copy of *Evangeline* annotated in French for the use of French children learning English at school; but whatever Longfellow's popularity in England or in Germany, he is really but little known in

France or Italy or Spain. With Goethe
and Schiller, with Scott and Byron, Cooper was one of the foreign forces which
brought about the Romanticist revolt in
France, profoundly affecting the literature
of all Latin countries. Dumas owed almost as much to Cooper as he did to
Scott ; and Balzac said that if Cooper had
only drawn character as well as he painted
" the phenomena of nature, he would have
uttered the last word of our art."

In his admirable life of Cooper, one of
the best of modern biographies, Professor
Lounsbury shows clearly the extraordinary state of affairs with which Cooper
had to contend. Foremost among the
disadvantages against which he had to
labor was the dull, deadening provincialism of American criticism at the time
when *The Spy* was written ; and as we
read Professor Lounsbury's pages we see
how bravely Cooper fought for our intellectual emancipation from the shackles
of the British criticism of that time, more
ignorant then and even more insular than
it is now. Abroad Cooper received the attention nearly always given in literature
to those who bring a new thing ; and the
new thing which Cooper annexed to liter-

ature was America. At home he had to struggle against a belief that our soil was barren of romance—as though the author who used his eyes could not find ample material wherever there was humanity. Cooper was the first who proved the fitness of American life and American history for the uses of fiction. *The Spy* is really the first of American novels, and it remains one of the best. Cooper was the prospector of that little army of industrious miners now engaged in working every vein of local color and character, and in sifting out the golden dust from the sands of local history. The authors of *Oldtown Folks*, of the *Tales of the Argonauts*, of *Old Creole Days*, and of *In the Tennessee Mountains* were but following in Cooper's footsteps — though they carried more modern tools. And when the desire of the day is for detail and for finish, it is not without profit to turn again to stories of a bolder sweep. When the tendency of the times is perhaps towards an undue elaboration of miniature portraits, there is gain in going back to the masterpieces of a literary artist who succeeded best in heroic statues. And not a few of us, whatever our code of literary esthetics, may find delight, fleeting though it be, in the free outline drawing of Cooper, after our eyes are tired by the niggling and cross-hatching of many among our contemporary realists. When our pleasant duty is done, when our examination is at an end, and when we seek to sum up our impressions and to set them down plainly, we find that chief among Cooper's characteristics were, first, a sturdy, hearty, robust, out-door and open-air wholesomeness, devoid of any trace of offence and free from all morbid taint ; and, secondly, an intense Americanism — ingrained, abiding, and dominant. Professor Lounsbury quotes from a British magazine of 1831 the statement that, to an Englishman, Cooper appeared to be prouder of his birth as an American than of his genius as an author — an attitude which may seem to some a little old-fashioned, but which on Cooper's part was both natural and becoming.

*The Spy* was the earliest of Cooper's American novels (and its predecessor, *Precaution*, a mere stencil imitation of the minor British novel of that day, need not be held in remembrance against him). *The Spy*, published in 1821, was followed in 1823 by *The Pioneers*, the first of the *Leatherstocking Tales* to appear, and by far the poorest ; indeed it is the only one of the five for which any apology need be made. The narrative drags under the burden of overabundant detail ; and the story may deserve to be called dull at times. Leatherstocking even is but a faint outline of himself, as the author afterwards with loving care elaborated the character. *The Last of the Mohicans* came out in 1826, and its success was instantaneous and enduring. In 1827 appeared *The Prairie*, the third tale in which Leatherstocking is the chief character. It is rare that an author is ever able to write a successful sequel to a successful story, yet Cooper did more; *The Prairie* is a sequel to *The Pioneers*, and *The Last of the Mohicans* is a prologue to it. Eighteen years after the first of the *Leatherstocking Tales* had been published, Cooper issued the last of them, amplifying his single sketch into a drama in five acts by the addition of *The Pathfinder*, printed in 1840, and of *The Deerslayer*, printed in 1841. In the sequence of events *The Deerslayer*, the latest written, is the earliest to be read; then comes *The Last of the Mohicans*, fol-

lowed by *The Pathfinder* and *The Pioneers;* while in *The Prairie* the series ends.
Of the incomparable variety of scene in
these five related tales, or of the extraordinary fertility of invention which they
reveal, it would not be easy to say too
much. In their kind they have never
been surpassed. The earliest to appear,
*The Pioneers*, is the least meritorious—as
though Cooper had not yet seen the value
of his material, and had not yet acquired
the art of handling it to advantage. *The
Pathfinder*, dignified as it is and pathetic
in its portrayal of Leatherstocking's love-
making, lacks the absorbing interest of
*The Last of the Mohicans;* it is perhaps
inferior in art to *The Deerslayer*, which
was written the year after, and it has not
the noble simplicity of *The Prairie*, in
which we see the end of the old hunter.

There are, no doubt, irregularities in
the *Leatherstocking Tales*, and the incon-
gruities and lesser errors inevitable in a
mode of composition at once desultory
and protracted; but there they stand, a
solid monument of American literature,
and not the least enduring. "If anything
from the pen of the writer of these romances is at all to outlive himself, it is,

unquestionably, the series of the *Leather-stocking Tales*"—so wrote the author when he sent forth the first collected and revised edition of the narrative of Natty Bumppo's adventures. That Cooper was right seems to-day indisputable. An author may fairly claim to be judged by his best, to be measured by his highest; and the *Leatherstocking Tales* are Cooper's highest and best in more ways than one, but chiefly because of the lofty figure of Leatherstocking. Lowell, when fabling for critics, said that Cooper had drawn but one new character, explaining afterwards that

The men who have given to *one* character life
And objective existence, are not very rife;
You may number them all, both prose-writers and sing-
    ers,
Without overruning the bounds of your fingers;
And Natty won't go to oblivion quicker
Than Adams the parson or Primrose the vicar.

And Thackeray—perhaps recalling the final scene in *The Prairie*, where the dying Leatherstocking drew himself up and said " Here !" and that other scene in *The Newcomes*, where the dying Colonel drew himself up and said " Adsum !"—was frequent in praise of Cooper; and in one of the *Roundabout Papers*, after expressing his fondness for Scott's modest and honorable heroes, he adds: "Much as I like these most unassuming, manly, unpretentious gentlemen, I have to own that I think the heroes of another writer—viz., Leatherstocking, Uncas, Hardheart, Tom Coffin—are quite the equals of Scott's men; perhaps Leatherstocking is better than any one in 'Scott's lot.' *La Longue Carabine* is one of the great prize-men of fiction. He ranks with your Uncle Toby, Sir Roger de Coverley, Falstaff—heroic figures all, American or British, and the artist has deserved well of his country who devised them."

It is to be noticed that Thackeray singled out for praise two of Cooper's Indians to pair with the hunter and the sailor; and it seems to me that Thackeray is fairer towards him who conceived Uncas and Hardheart than are the authors of *A Fable for Critics* and of *Condensed Novels*. *Muck-a-Muck* I should set aside among the parodies which are unfair—so far as the red man is concerned, at least; for I hold as quite fair Mr. Harte's raillery of the wooden maidens and polysyllabic old men who stalk through Cooper's pages.

7

Cooper's Indian has been disputed and he has been laughed at, but he still lives. Cooper's Indian is very like Mr. Parkman's Indian—and who knows the red man better than the author of *The Oregon Trail?* Uncas and Chingachgook and Hardheart are all good men and true, and June, the wife of Arrowhead, the Tuscarora, is a good wife and a true woman. They are Indians, all of them; heroic figures, no doubt, and yet taken from life, with no more idealization than may serve the maker of romance. They remind us that when West first saw the Apollo Belvedere he thought at once of a Mohawk brave. They were the result of knowledge and of much patient investigation under conditions forever passed away. We see Cooper's Indians nowadays through mists of prejudice due to those who have imitated them from the outside. *The Last of the Mohicans* has suffered the degradation of a trail of dime novels, written by those apparently more familiar with the Five Points than with the Five Nations; Cooper begat Mayne Reid, and Mayne Reid begat Ned Buntline and *Buffalo Bill's First Scalp for Custer* and similar abominations. But none the less are Uncas and Hardheart noble figures, worthily drawn, and never to be mentioned without praise.

In 1821 Cooper published *The Spy*, the first American historical novel; in 1823 he published *The Pioneers*, in which the backwoodsman and the red man were first introduced into literature; and in 1824 he published *The Pilot*, and for the first time the scene of a story was laid on the sea rather than on the land, and the interest turned wholly on marine adventure. In four years Cooper had put forth three novels, each in its way road-breaking and epoch-making: only the great men of letters have a record like this. With the recollection before us of some of Smollett's highly colored naval characters, we cannot say that Cooper sketched the first real sailor in fiction, but he invented the sea tale just as Poe invented the detective story—and in neither case has any disciple surpassed the master. The supremacy of the *The Pilot* and *The Red Rover* is quite as evident as the supremacy of the *The Gold Bug* and *The Murders in the Rue Morgue*. We have been used to the novel of the ocean, and it is hard for us now to understand why

Cooper's friends thought his attempt to write one perilous and why they sought to dissuade him. It was believed that readers could not be interested in the contingencies and emergencies of life on the ocean wave. Nowadays it seems to us that if any part of *The Pilot* lags and stumbles it is that which passes ashore : Cooper's landscapes, or at least his views of a ruined abbey, may be affected at times, but his marines are always true and always captivating.

Cooper, like Thackeray, forbade his family to authorize or aid any biographer —although the American novelist had as little to conceal as the English. No doubt Cooper had his faults, both as a man and as an author. He was thin-skinned and hot-headed. He let himself become involved in a great many foolish quarrels. He had a plentiful lack of tact. But the man was straightforward and high-minded, and so was the author. We can readily pardon his petty pedantries and the little vices of expression he persisted in. We can confess that his "females," as he would term them, are indubitably wooden. We may acknowledge that even among his men there is no wide range of character;

Richard Jones (in *The Pioneers*) is first cousin to Cap (in *The Pathfinder*), just as Long Tom Coffin is a half-brother of Natty Bumppo. We must admit that Cooper's lighter characters are not touched with the humor that Scott could command at will; the Naturalist (in *The Prairie*), for example, is not alive and delightful like the Antiquary of Scott.

In the main, indeed, Cooper's humor is not of the purest. When he attempted it of malice prepense it was often laboriously unfunny. But sometimes, as it fell accidentally from the lips of Leatherstocking, it was unforced and delicious (see, for instance, at the end of chapter xxvii. of *The Pathfinder*, the account of Natty's sparing the sleeping Mingos and of the fate which thereafter befell them at the hands of Chingachgook). On the other hand, Cooper's best work abounds in fine romantic touches — Long Tom pinning the British captain to the mast with the harpoon, the wretched Abiram (in *The Prairie*) tied hand and foot and left on a ledge with a rope around his neck so that he can move only to hang himself, the death-grip of the brave (in *The Last of the Mohicans*) hanging wounded and without hope over the watery abyss—these are pictures fixed in the memory and now unforgetable.

Time is unerring in its selection. Cooper has now been dead nearly two-score years. What survives of his work are the *Sea Tales* and the *Leatherstocking Tales*. From these I have found myself forced to cite characters and episodes. These are the stories which hold their own in the libraries. Public and critics are at one here. The wind of the lakes and the prairies has not lost its balsam, and the salt of the sea keeps its savor. For the free movement of his figures and for the proper expansion of his story Cooper needed a broad region and a widening vista. He excelled in conveying the suggestion of vastness and limitless space, and of depicting the human beings proper to these great reaches of land and water —the two elements he ruled ; and he was equally at home on the rolling waves of the prairie and on the green and irregular hillocks of the ocean.

1889

"IN the four quarters of the globe, who reads an American book?" asked Sydney Smith in the *Edinburgh Review*, in 1820; and for years the American people writhed under the query as though they had been put to the question themselves. In those days the American cuticle was extraordinarily sensitive, and the gentlest stroke of satire caused exquisite pain. But although Sydney Smith was unkind, he was not unjust; in the four quarters of the globe nobody to-day reads any American book published before 1820—except Irving's *Knickerbocker*. In the very year that Sydney Smith wrote there was published in England a book which might have arrested the dean's sarcastic inquiry had it appeared a few months earlier. This was Irving's *Sketch Book*. The Americans of seventy years ago did not know it; but none the less is it a fact that American literature made a very poor showing then, and that there was in existence in those days scarcely a single book with vitality enough to survive threescore years and ten. The men who were to make our literature what it is were then alive—Irving, Cooper, Bryant, Emerson, Longfellow, Whittier, Holmes, Lowell, Poe, Hawthorne, Bancroft, Prescott, and Motley; but Irving's *Knickerbocker* was the only book then in print which to-day is read or readable. It was only in 1821 that Cooper published the *Spy*, the first American historical novel, and the first of the *Leatherstocking Tales* did not appear until 1823. Reverberations of the angry roar which answered Sydney Smith's question must have reached his ears, for, in 1824, again in the *Edinburgh Review*, he wondered at our touchiness: " That Americans . . . should be flung into such convulsions by English Reviewers and Magazines is really a sad specimen of Columbian juvenility."

Now we have changed all that. In less than three-quarters of a century (a very short time in the history of a nation)

our cuticle has toughened—perhaps the
process was hastened by the strokes of a
long war fought for conscience' sake. It
is not so easy now to wring our withers,
and more often than not it is on the other
side of the Atlantic that the galled jade
winces. John Bull is not as pachyder-
matous as once he was, and a chance
word of Brother Jonathan's penetrates
and rankles. Mr. Charles Dudley Warner
once let fall an innocent remark about the
British strawberry; and more than one
British journal flushed with rage till it
rivalled the redness of that worthy but
hollow-hearted fruit. Mr. W. D. Howells
suggested a criticism of two British novelists; and the editor of the *Saturday Review* made ready to accept the command
of the Channel Fleet. Mr. Theodore
Roosevelt rebuked a British general for
insulting Robert E. Lee with blundering
laudation; and Mr. Andrew Lang promptly wrote a paper on " International Girl-
ishness," in which he very courteously offered himself as an example of the failing
he described. In a little essay on the centenary of Fenimore Cooper, I remarked
that the reader of Professor Lounsbury's
admirable biography could " see how

bravely Cooper fought for our intellectual emancipation from the shackles of the British criticism of that time, more ignorant then and even more insular than it is now;" and against this casual accusation that British criticism is or was ignorant and insular, Mr. Andrew Lang again protested, with his wonted suavity, of course, but with energy nevertheless and with emphasis.

Turn about is fair enough. When Time plays the fiddle, the dancers must needs change places; and we Americans have no call for weeping that the British attitude to-day resembles ours in the early part of the century more than our own does. The change is pleasant, and Mr. Andrew Lang ought not to object to our enjoyment of it. As regards the special charge that British criticism was more ignorant and more insular fifty odd years ago than it is now—well, I do not think that Mr. Andrew Lang ought to object to that either. If I understand my own statement, it means that there has been an improvement in British criticism in the past half-century; and I do not think that this assertion affords a fair ground for a quarrel. Still, when Mr. Andrew

Lang throws down the gauntlet, I cannot
refuse to put on the gloves; and I decline
to avail myself of the small side door he
kindly left ajar for my escape.

First, it is to be noted that when Mr.
Andrew Lang writes about "critics," and
when I wrote, we were discussing different
things. There are two kinds of critics,
and the word criticism may mean either
of two things. The writer of an anonymous book-review printed in a daily or
weekly paper considers himself a critic,
and the product of his pen is accepted as a
criticism. But there is no other word than
criticism to describe the finest work (in
prose) of James Russell Lowell and of
Matthew Arnold. Mr. Andrew Lang
chooses to consider chiefly what might be
called the higher criticism, and he sets
aside the lower critics as " reviewers," declaring that " reviewers are rarely critics, and they are often very tired, very
casual, very flippant." Now, it was this
sort of British critic, the very casual
and very flippant reviewer, that I meant
when I spoke of the ignorance and insularity of British criticism; and it was
the attitude of British critics of this type
towards America that I had in mind. It

was to their ignorance of America and Americans that I referred, and to the insularity of their position towards us. This ignorance is now less than it was in Cooper's time, and of late the insularity has been modified for the better. But that they were "very tired, very casual, and very flippant" is not an excuse for their constant attitude towards most American authors; it is not even an adequate reason. No doubt Mr. Andrew Lang knows the anecdote—is there any Merry Jest that he has not heard?—of the Judge who chafed under the insulting demeanor of a certain barrister until at last he was forced to protest: "Brother Blank," he said, "I know my great inferiority to you; but, after all, I am a vertebrate animal, and your manner towards me would be unbecoming from God Almighty to a black beetle!"

It is in relation to America and to American workers that we find British criticism ignorant and insular. The ordinary British critic assumes a very different tone towards us from that he assumes towards the French or the Germans. He may dislike these, but he accepts them as equals. Us he regards as

inferiors—as degenerate Englishmen unfortunately cut off from communion with
the father-land and the mother-tongue,
and to be chided because we do not
humbly acknowledge our deficiencies.
He does not know that we are now
no more English than the English themselves are now Germans. He does not
guess that we are proud that we are not
English—prouder, perhaps, of nothing else.
He does not think that we do not like
being treated as though we were younger
sons in exile—wandering prodigals, deserving no better fare than the husks
of patronizing criticism. No American
likes to be patronized, and even some
Englishmen seem to object to it; apparently Mr. Andrew Lang did not approve of
the critical nepotism of a certain Teutonic
reviewer. But the lordliness of the eminent German who reviewed Mr. Andrew
Lang's book without reading it was tem-
pered by the good faith with which he
confessed his ignorance; and his offence
was less heinous than that of the critic in
the *Saturday Review*, who dismissed Mr.
Aldrich's "Queen of Sheba" with a curt
assertion that it was like the author's other
poems.

As the Greek felt towards the Barbarian and as the Jew towards the Gentile, so does the ordinary British critic feel towards America. The feeling of the Greek and of the Jew was perhaps based on a serious reason ; but what justifies the lofty superiority of the British critic? Is not its cause the self-satisfaction of ignorant insularity?—using neither word in any offensive sense. And does it not result in a willingness to condemn without knowledge and without any effort to acquire knowledge? Any one who recalls Brougham's review of Byron's first book, or Jeffrey's attack on Keats, or Wilson's dissection of Tennyson, knows that there are British criticisms which are not models of sweetness and light; never are sweetness and light more frequently absent than in British criticism of America and of Americans. "Light," I take it, means knowledge; and "sweetness" is incompatible with that form of *morgue britannique* which one may call insularity.

The higher criticism in England, which Mr. Andrew Lang praises perhaps not more than it deserves, has developed greatly within the last twenty years. It is not ignorant like the very tired, very casual, and very flippant reviewing, nor in the same fashion ; but it has an ignorance of its own, compounded of many simples. Its attitude towards us is not as offensive, but it is not without its touch of superiority now and again. Mr. Andrew Lang himself, for example, is ignorant of our best critics, and confesses his ignorance as frankly as did his Teutonic reviewer ; and then he reveals what is not wholly unlike insularity in his readiness, despite this ignorance, to make comparisons between American critics and British.

On Mr. Andrew Lang's list of British critics are the names of Mr. Ruskin, Mr. J. A. Symonds, Mr. R. L. Stevenson, Mr. Leslie Stephen, Mr. Walter Pater, Mr. George Saintsbury, Mr. Frederic Harrison, Professor Robertson Smith, Mr. Swinburne, and Mr. Theodore Watts—and every reader must instinctively add Mr. Andrew Lang's own name to a list on which it will find no superior. The list seems oddly chosen ; an American misses the name of Mr. John Morley, perhaps the foremost of British critics of our day, and those of Mr. Austin Dobson, and of Mr. William Archer. Of American critics

Mr. Andrew Lang can recall of his own
accord, apparently, only the name of Lowell, and he remarks that " Mr. Howells, in
an essay on this subject, mentions Mr.
Stedman and Mr. T. S. Perry, doubtless
with justice." If there were any advantage in making out a list of American critics to place beside the list of British critics, I should put down the names of Mr.
Curtis, Col. Higginson, Mr. Warner, Mr.
R. H. Stoddard, Professor Lounsbury,
Professor T. F. Crane, Mr. W. C. Brownell, Mr. John Burroughs, Mr. George E.
Woodberry, and Mr. Henry James—add-
ing, of course, the names of Mr. Stedman
and of Professor Child, mentioned by Mr.
Andrew Lang in another part of his paper. But I fear me greatly that this is
idle; it is but the setting up of one personal equation over against another. Or-
thodoxy is my doxy and heterodoxy is
your doxy. Counting of noses is not the
best way to settle a dispute about literature.

Indeed there is no way to settle such a
dispute, and there is no hope of coming to
an agreement. "It is a very pretty quarrel as it stands;" and if "we quarrel in
print, by the book," let us stop at the first

degree, the Retort Courteous, not going
on even to the third, the Reply Churlish.
Also is there much virtue in an If. " If
you said so, then I said so."   Let us then,
while there is yet time, shake hands
across the Atlantic and swear brothers.

1890

8

OUBTLESS criticism was originally benignant, pointing out the beauties of a work rather than its defects. The passions of man have made it malignant, as the bad heart of Procrustes turned the bed, the symbol of repose, into an instrument of torture." So wrote Longfellow a many years ago, thinking, it may be, on *English Bards and Scotch Reviewers*, or on the Jedburgh justice of Jeffrey. But we may question whether the poet did not unduly idealize the past, as is the custom of poets, and whether he did not unfairly asperse the present. With the general softening of manners, no doubt those of the critic have improved also. Surely, since a time whereof the memory of man runneth not to the contrary, " to criticise," in the ears of many, if not of most, has been synonymous with " to find fault." In Farquhar's ' Inconstant," now nearly two hundred years old, Petit says of a certain lady: " She's a critic, sir ; she hates a jest, for fear it should please her."

The critics themselves are to blame for this misapprehension of their attitude. When Mr. Arthur Pendennis wrote reviews for the *Pall Mall Gazette*, he settled the poet's claims as though he " were my lord on the bench and the author a miserable little suitor trembling before him." The critic of this sort acts not only as judge and jury, first finding the author guilty and then putting on the black cap to sentence him to the gallows, but he often volunteers as executioner also, laying on a round dozen lashes with his own hand, and with a hearty good-will. We are told, for example, that Captain Shandon knew the crack of Warrington's whip and the cut his thong left. Bludyer went to work like a butcher and mangled his subject, but Warrington finished a man, laying " his cuts neat and regular, straight down the back, and drawing blood every time."

Whenever I recall this picture I understand the protest of one of the most acute

and subtle of American critics, who told
me that he did not much mind what was
said about his articles so long as they
were not called "trenchant." Perhaps
trenchant is the adjective which best de-
fines what true criticism is not. True
criticism, so Joubert tells us, is *un ex-
ercice méthodique de discernement.* It is
an effort to understand and to explain.
The true critic is no more an executioner
than he is an assassin; he is rather a seer,
sent forward to spy out the land, and most
useful when he comes back bringing a good
report and bearing a full cluster of grapes.

*La critique sans bonté trouble le gout
et empoisonne les saveurs,* said Joubert
again; unkindly criticism disturbs the
taste and poisons the savor. No one of
the great critics was unkindly. That Macaulay mercilessly flayed Montgomery is
evidence, were any needed, that Macaulay was not one of the great critics. The
tomahawk and the scalping-knife are not
the critical apparatus, and they are not to
be found in the armory of Lessing and of
Sainte-Beuve, of Matthew Arnold and of
James Russell Lowell. It is only inci-
dentally that these devout students of
letters find fault. Though they may ban

now and again, they came to bless. They
chose their subjects, for the most part, because they loved these, and were eager to
praise them and to make plain to the
world the reasons for their ardent affection. Whenever they might chance to
see incompetence and pretension pushing
to the front, they shrugged their shoulders more often than not, and passed by
on the other side silently :—and so best.
Very rarely did they cross over to expose
an impostor.

Lessing waged war upon theories of art,
but he kept up no fight with individual authors. Sainte-Beuve sought to paint the
portrait of the man as he was, warts and
all; but he did not care for a sitter who
was not worth the most loving art. Matthew Arnold was swift to find the joints
in his opponent's armor; but there is
hardly one of his essays in criticism which
had not its exciting cause in his admiration for its subject. Mr. Lowell has not
always hidden his scorn of a sham, and
sometimes he has scourged it with a single sharp phrase. Generally, however,
even the humbugs get off scot-free, for
the true critic knows that time will at-
tend to these fellows, and there is rarely

any need to lend a hand. It was Bentley who said that no man was ever written down save by himself.

The late Edouard Scherer once handled M. Emile Zola without gloves; and M. Jules Lemaître has made M. Georges Ohnet the target of his flashing wit. But each of these attacks attained notoriety from its unexpectedness. And what has been gained in either case? Since Scherer fell foul of him, M. Zola has written his strongest novel, *Germinal* (one of the most powerful tales of this century), and his rankest story, *La Terre* (one of the most offensive fictions in all the history of literature). M. Lemaître's brilliant assault on M. Ohnet may well have excited pity for the wretched victim; and, damaging as it was, I doubt if its effect is as fatal as the gentler and more humorous criticism of M. Anatole France, in which the reader sees contempt slowly gaining the mastery over the honest critic's kindliness.

For all that he was a little prim in taste and a little arid in manner, Scherer had the gift of appreciation—the most precious possession of any critic. M. Lemaître, despite his frank enjoyment of his own

skill in fence, has a faculty of hearty admiration. There are thirteen studies in
the first series of his *Contemporains*, and
the dissection of the unfortunate M. Ohnet is the only one in which the critic
does not handle his scalpel with loving
care. To run amuck through the throng
of one's fellow-craftsmen is not a sign of
sanity—on the contrary. Depreciation is
cheaper than appreciation; and criticism
which is merely destructive is essentially
inferior to criticism which is constructive.
That he saw so little to praise is greatly
against Poe's claim to be taken seriously
as a critic; so is his violence of speech;
and so also is the fact that those whom he
lauded might be as little deserving of his
eulogy as those whom he assailed were
worthy of his condemnation. The habit of
intemperate attack which grew on Poe is
foreign to the serene calm of the higher
criticism. F. D. Maurice made the shrewd
remark that the critics who take pleasure
in cutting up mean books soon deteriorate
themselves — subdued to that they work
in. It may be needful, once in a way, to
nail vermin to the barn door as a warning,
and thus we may seek a reason for Macaulay's cruel treatment of Montgomery,

and M. Lemaître's pitiless castigation of M. Ohnet. But in nine cases out of ten, or rather in ninety-nine out of a hundred, the attitude of the critic towards contemporary trash had best be one of absolute indifference, sure that Time will sift out what is good, and that Time winnows with unerring taste.

The duty of the critic, therefore, is to help the reader to "get the best"—in the old phrase of the dictionary venders—to choose it, to understand it, to enjoy it. To choose it, first of all; so must the critic dwell with delighted insistence upon the best books, drawing attention afresh to the old and discovering the new with alert vision. Neglect is the proper portion of the worthless books of the hour, whatever may be their vogue for the week or the month. It cannot be declared too frequently that temporary popularity is no sure test of real merit; else were *Proverbial Philosophy*, the *Light of Asia*, and the *Epic of Hades* the foremost British poems since the decline of Robert Montgomery; else were the *Lamplighter* (does any one read the *Lamplighter* nowadays, I wonder?), *Looking Backward*, and *Mr. Barnes of New York* the typical American

novels. No one can insist too often on
the distinction between what is "good
enough" for current consumption by a
careless public and what is really good,
permanent, and secure. No one can declare with too much emphasis the difference between what is literature and what
is not literature, nor the width of the gulf
which separates them. A critic who has
not an eye single to this distinction fails
of his duty. Perhaps the best way to
make the distinction plain to the reader
is to persist in discussing what is vital and
enduring, pointedly passing over what may
happen to be accidentally popular.

Yet the critic mischooses who should
shut himself up with the classics of all
languages and in rapt contemplation of
their beauties be blind to the best work
of his own time. If criticism itself is to
be seen of men, it must enter the arena
and bear a hand in the combat. The
books which have come down to us from
our fathers and from our grandfathers are
a blessed heritage, no doubt; but there
are a few books of like value to be picked
out of those which we of to-day shall pass
along to our children and to our grand-
children. It may be even that some of

our children are beginning already to set
down in black and white their impressions
of life, with a skill and with a truth which
shall in due season make them classics
also. Sainte-Beuve asserted that the real
triumph of the critic was when the poets
whose praises he had sounded and for
whom he had fought grew in stature and
surpassed themselves, keeping, and more
than keeping, the magnificent promises
which the critic, as their sponsor in bap-
tism, had made for them. Besides the
criticism of the classics, grave, learned,
definitive, there is another more alert, said
Sainte - Beuve, more in touch with the
spirit of the hour, more lightly equipped,
it may be, and yet more willing to find
answers for the questions of the day.
This more vivacious criticism chooses
its heroes and encompasses them about
with its affection, using boldly the words
"genius" and "glory," however much
this may scandalize the lookers-on :

> "Nous tiendrons, pour lutter dans l'arène lyrique,
>     Toi la lance, moi les coursiers."

To few critics is it given to prophesy
the lyric supremacy of a Victor Hugo—it
was in a review of *Les Feuilles d'Automne*

that Sainte-Beuve made this declaration
of principles. A critic lacking the insight and the equipment of Sainte-Beuve
may unduly despise an Ugly Duckling, or
he may mistake a Goose for a Swan, only
to wait in vain for its song. Indeed, to
set out of malice prepense to discover a
genius is but a wild-goose chase at best ;
and though the sport is pleasant for those
who follow, it may be fatal to the chance
fowl who is expected to lay a golden egg.
Longfellow's assertion that "critics are
sentinels in the grand army of letters,
stationed at the corners of newspapers
and reviews to challenge every new author," may not be altogether acceptable,
but it is at least the duty of the soldier
to make sure of the papers of those who
seek to enlist in the garrison.

" British criticism has always been more
or less parochial," said Lowell, many years
ago, before he had been American Min-
ister at St. James's. " It cannot quite
persuade itself that truth is of immortal
essence, totally independent of all assistance from quarterly journals or the British army and navy." No doubt there has
been a decided improvement in the temper
of British criticism since this was written ;

it is less parochial than it was, and it is perhaps now one of its faults that it affects a cosmopolitanism to which it does not attain. But even now an American of literary taste is simply staggered—there is no other word for it—whenever he reads the weekly reviews of contemporary fiction in the *Athenæum*, the *Academy*, the *Spectator*, and the *Saturday Review*, and when he sees high praise bestowed on novels so poor that no American pirate imperils his salvation to reprint them. The encomiums bestowed, for example, upon such tales as those which are written by the ladies who call themselves "Rita" and "The Duchess" and "The Authoress of *The House on the Marsh*," seem hopelessly uncritical. The writers of most of these reviews are sadly lacking in literary perception and in literary perspective. The readers of these reviews—if they had no other sources of information—would never suspect that the novel of England is no longer what it was once, and that it is now inferior in art to the novel of France, of Spain, and of America. If the petty minnows are magnified thus, what lens will serve fitly to reproduce the lordly salmon or the stal-

wart tarpon? Those who praise the second-rate or the tenth-rate in terms appropriate only to the first-rate are derelict
to the first duty of the critic—which is to
help the reader to choose the best.

And the second duty of the critic is
like unto the first. It is to help the reader to understand the best. There is many
a book which needs to be made plain to
him who runs as he reads, and it is the
running reader of these hurried years that
the critic must needs address. There are
not a few works of high merit (although
none, perhaps, of the very highest) which
gain by being explained, even as Philip
expounded Esaias to the eunuch of Can-
dace, Queen of the Ethiopians, getting
up into his chariot and guiding him.
Perhaps it is paradoxical to suggest that
a book of the very highest class is perforce clear beyond all need of commen-
tary or exposition; but it is indisputable
that familiarity may blur the outline and
use may wear away the sharp edges, until
we no longer see the masterpiece as distinctly as we might, nor do we regard it
with the same interest. Here again the
critic finds his opportunity; he may show
the perennial freshness of that which

seemed for a while withered; and he may interpret again the meaning of the message an old book may bring to a new generation. Sometimes this message is valuable and yet invisible from the outside, like the political pamphlets which were smuggled into the France of the Second Empire concealed in the hollow plaster busts of Napoleon III., but ready to the hand that knew how to extract them adroitly at the proper time.

The third duty of the critic, after aiding the reader to choose the best and to understand it, is to help him to enjoy it. This is possible only when the critic's own enjoyment is acute enough to be contagious. However well informed a critic may be, and however keen he may be, if he be not capable of the cordial admiration which warms the heart, his criticism is wanting. A critic whose enthusiasm is not catching lacks the power of disseminating his opinions. His judgment may be excellent, but his influence remains negative. One torch may light many a fire; and how far a little candle throws its beams! Perhaps the ability to take an intense delight in another man's work, and the willingness to express this delight frankly

and fully, are two of the characteristics
of the true critic; of a certainty they are
the characteristics most frequently absent in the criticaster. Consider how
Sainte-Beuve and Matthew Arnold and
Lowell have sung the praises of those
whose poems delighted them. Note how
Mr. Henry James and M. Jules Lemaître
are affected by the talents of M. Al-
phonse Daudet and of M. Guy de Mau-
passant.

Having done his duty to the reader,
the critic has done his full duty to the
author also. It is to the people at large
that the critic is under obligations, not to
any individual. As he cannot take cog-
nizance of a work of art, literary or dramatic, plastic or pictorial, until after it is
wholly complete, his opinion can be of
little benefit to the author. A work of
art is finally finished when it comes before
the public, and the instances are very few
indeed when an author has ever thought
it worth while to modify the form in
which it was first presented to the world.
A work of science, on the other hand,
depending partly on the exactness of the
facts which it sets forth and on which it
is founded, may gain from the suggested

emendations of a critic. Many a history, many a law book, many a scientific treatise has been bettered in successive editions by hints gleaned here and there from the reviews of experts.

But the work of art stands on a wholly different footing from the work of science; and the critics have no further duty towards the author, except, of course, to treat him fairly, and to present him to the public if they deem him worthy of this honor. The novel or the poem being done once for all, it is hardly possible for critics to be of any use to the novelist or to the poet personally. The artist of experience makes up his mind to this, and accepts criticism as something which has little or nothing to do with his work, but which may materially affect his position before the public. Thackeray, who understood the feelings and the failings of the literary man as no one else, has shown us Mr. Arthur Pendennis reading the newspaper notices of his novel, *Walter Lorraine*, and sending them home to his mother. "Their censure did not much affect him; for the good-natured young man was disposed to accept with considerable humility the dispraise of others.

Nor did their praise elate him overmuch;
for, like most honest persons, he had his
own opinion about his own performance,
and when a critic praised him in the wrong
place he was hurt rather than pleased by
the compliment."

Mr. James tells us that the author of
*Smoke* and *Fathers and Sons*, a far greater
novelist than the author of *Walter Lorraine*, had a serene indifference towards
criticism. Turgenef gave Mr. James "the
impression of thinking of criticism as
most serious workers think of it—that it
is the amusement, the exercise, the sub-
sistence of the critic (and, so far as this
goes, of immense use), but that, though
it may often concern other readers, it
does not much concern the artist himself."
Though criticism is of little use to the
author directly, it can be of immense service to him indirectly, if it be exposition
rather than comment; not a bald and
barren attempt at classification, but a
sympathetic interpretation. At bottom,
sympathy is the prime requisite of the
critic; and with sympathy come appreciation, penetration, revelation—such, for
example, as the American novelist has
shown in his criticisms of the Russian.

9

There is one kind of review of no benefit either to the author or to the public.
This is the careless, perfunctory book-no-
tice, penned hastily by a tired writer, who
does not take the trouble to formulate his
opinion, and perhaps not even to form one.
Towards the end of 1889 there appeared
in a British weekly the following notice
of a volume of American short stories:

"A littery gent in one of Mr. [——]'s short stories
says: 'A good idea for a short story is a shy bird, and
doesn't come for the calling.' Alas! alas! it is true.
The French can call a great deal better than we can;
but the Americans, it would seem, cannot. The best of
Mr. [——]'s stories is the first, about a tree which grew
out of the bosom of a buried suicide, and behaved accord-
ingly to his descendants; but, so far from being a short
story, it is a long one, extending over some hundreds of
years, and it suffers from the compression which Mr.
[——] puts upon it. It deserves to have a volume to itself."

Refraining from all remark upon the
style in which this paragraph is written
or upon the taste of the writer, I desire
to call attention to the fact that it is not
what it purports to be. It is not a criticism within the accepted meaning of the
word. It indicates no intellectual effort
on the part of its writer to understand the
author of the book. An author would
need to be superlatively sensitive who

could take offence at this paragraph, and an author who could find pleasure in it would have to be unspeakably vain. To me this notice seems the absolute negation of criticism — mere words with no suggestion of a thought behind them. The man who dashed this off robbed the author of a criticism to which he was entitled if the book was worth reviewing at all; and in thus shirking his bounden duty he also cheated the proprietor of the paper who paid him. Empty paragraphing of this offensive character is commoner now than it was a few years ago, commoner in Great Britain than in the United States, and commoner in anonymous articles than in those warranted by the signature of the writer. Probably the man who was guilty of this innocuous notice would have been ashamed to put his name to it.

If a book is so empty that there is nothing to say about it, then there is no need to say anything. It is related that when a dramatist, who was reading a play before the Committee of the Comédie Française, rebuked M. Got for slumbering peacefully during this ceremony, the eminent comedian answered promptly, "Sleep,

Monsieur, is also an opinion." If a book puts the critic to sleep, or so benumbs his faculties that he finds himself speechless, he has no call to proceed further in the matter. Perhaps the author may take heart of grace when he remembers that of all Shakespeare's characters, it was the one with the ass's head who had an exposition of sleep come upon him, as it was the one with the blackest heart who said he was nothing if not critical.

If I were to attempt to draw up Twelve Good Rules for Reviewers, I should begin with:

I. Form an honest opinion.

II. Express it honestly.

III. Don't review a book which you cannot take seriously.

IV. Don't review a book with which you are out of sympathy. That is to say, put yourself in the author's place, and try to see his work from his point of view, which is sure to be a coign of vantage.

V. Stick to the text. Review the book before you, and not the book some other author might have written; *obiter dicta* are as valueless from the critic as from the judge. Don't go off on a tangent. And also don't go round in a circle. Say what you have to say, and stop. Don't go on writing about and about the subject, and merely weaving garlands of flowers of rhetoric.

VI. Beware of the Sham Sample, as Charles Reade called it. Make sure that the specimen bricks you select for quotation do not give a false impression of the *façade*, and not only of the elevation merely, but of the perspective also, and of the ground-plan.

VII. In reviewing a biography or a history, criticise the book before you, and don't write a parallel essay, for which the volume you have in hand serves only as a peg.

VIII. In reviewing a work of fiction, don't give away the plot. In the eyes of the novelist this is the unpardonable sin. And, as it discounts the pleasure of the reader also, it is almost equally unkind to him.

IX. Don't try to prove every successful author a plagiarist. It may be that many a successful author has been a plagiarist, but no author ever succeeded because of his plagiary.

X. Don't break a butterfly on a wheel. If a book is not worth much, it is not worth reviewing.

XI. Don't review a book as an east wind would review an apple-tree—so it was once said Douglas Jerrold was wont to do. Of what profit to any one is mere bitterness and vexation of spirit?

XII. Remember that the critic's duty is to the reader mainly, and that it is to guide him not only to what is good, but to what is best. Three parts of what is contemporary must be temporary only.

Having in the past now and again fallen from grace myself and written criticism, I know that on such occasions these Twelve Good Rules would have been exceedingly helpful to me had I then possessed them; therefore I offer them now hopefully to my fellow-critics. But I find myself in a state of humility (to which few critics are accustomed), and I doubt how far my good advice will be heeded. I remember that, after reporting the speech in which Poor Richard's maxims were all massed together, Franklin tells us that "thus the old gentleman ended his harangue. The people heard it and approved the doctrine; and immediately practised the contrary, just as if it had been a common sermon."

1890

HOEVER wishes to attain an English style, familiar but not coarse, and elegant but not ostentatious, must give his days and nights to the study of Addison," said Doctor Johnson a many years ago ; and Doctor Johnson's own style, elaborate if not artificial, and orotund if not polysyllabic, might no doubt have been improved if the writer of the *Rambler* had given more of his days and nights to the study of the chief writer of the *Spectator*. Doctor Johnson's advice is still quoted often, perhaps it is still followed sometimes. Yet it is outworn and not for to-day. We have nowadays better weapons than the Brown Bess Johnson appreciated so highly—breech-loading rifles incomparably superior to the smooth-bore he praises. Owing in part, no doubt, to the influence

of Addison and to the advice of Johnson,
we have had writers of late whose style
is easier than Addison's, more graceful,
more varied, more precise. Set a page
of one of Addison's little apologues beside a page of one of Hawthorne's tales,
and note how much more pellucid Hawthorne's style is, how much more beauti-
ful, how much more distinguished. Contrast one of Addison's criticisms with one
of Matthew Arnold's, and observe not
only how much more complete is the terminology of the art now than it was when
the *Spectator* was appearing twice a week,
but also how much more acute and how
much more flexible the mind of the later
critic than the mind of the earlier.

Compare Addison's essays with those
which Mr. George William Curtis has recently collected into a volume, *From the
Easy Chair*, and you will see no reason to
adopt any theory of literary degeneracy
in our day. We are all of us the heirs
of the ages, no doubt, but it is in an unusual degree that Mr. Curtis is the inher-
itor of the best traditions of the English essay. He is the direct descendant
of Addison, whose style is overrated; of
Steele, whose morality is humorous; of

Goldsmith, whose writing was angelic, and of Irving, whose taste was pretty. Mr. Curtis recalls all of these, yet he is like none of them. Humorous as they are and charming, he is somewhat sturdier, of a more robust fibre, with a stronger respect for plain living and high thinking, with a firmer grasp on the duties of life.

For the most part these essays of Mr. Curtis's are pleasant papers of reminiscence, of gentle moralizing, and of kindly satire; but he is a swift and a careless reader who does not detect the underlying preachment which is at the core of most of them. Mr. Curtis is not content to scourge lightly the snobbery and the vulgarity which cling to the fringe of fashion, and sometimes get nearer to the centre of society; he also sets up a high standard of morality in public life. The divorce between Politics and Society—in the narrower meaning of the words—is not wholesome for either party. Mr. Curtis reminds us that "good government is one of the best things in the world," and that the wise man "knows that good things of that kind are not cheap." This is a quotation from the highly instructive and permanently pertinent paper on "Honestus at the Caucus," which begins with the assertion that "a man who is easily discouraged, who is not willing to put the good seed out of sight and wait for results, who desponds if he cannot obtain everything at once, and who thinks the human race lost if he is disappointed, will be very unhappy if he persists in taking part in politics. There is no sphere in which self-deception is easier."

There are but few essays with a political intention in this delightful little book. The rest are papers mainly about people, about " Edward Everett in 1862," and about " Emerson Lecturing," and about " Dickens Reading," and about " Robert Browning in Florence," and about "Wendell Phillips at Harvard," and about " A Little Dinner with Thackeray," and about Thoreau, who had " a staccato style of speech, every word coming separately and distinctly as if preserving the same cool isolation in the sentence that the speaker did in society." Not a few of them have to do with the players of the past, with the vocalists who are now but memories of dead and gone delight, with the performers on musical instruments—" Thal-

berg and other Pianists," "At the Opera in
1864," "Jenny Lind." Was the gentle Jenny Lind really a vocalist, or was she only a
singer of songs, unforgetable now because
she sang them? As we read these re-
minders of past delights we find ourselves
wondering how Jenny Lind would please
the denizens of certain Unmusical Boxes
at the Metropolitan Opera-house, "who
have an insatiable desire to proceed with
their intellectual cultivation by audible
conversation during the performance."

In the thick of the tussle of life here
in this huge city of ours, where strident
voices fill the market-place, the mellow
note of the essayist is heard distinctly as
he leans back in his Easy Chair, modu-
lating every syllable with exquisite felicity. And perhaps the author of the
*Potiphar Papers* is in his way quite as
characteristic of New York as any of the
more self-seeking notorieties who din
into our ears the catalogue of their merits. In a great city there is room for all,
for the boss and the heeler and the tough,
as well as for the *Tatler*, the *Spectator*,
the *Idler*, the *Rambler*, and the *Citizen
of the World*.

A citizen of the world, Mr. Curtis is,

beyond all question, really cosmopolitan; and, as Colonel Higginson told us a dozen years ago, "to be really cosmopolitan a man must be at home even in his own country." When Colonel Higginson came to New York last year to deliver before the Nineteenth Century Club the lecture on *The New World and the New Book*, which gives its title to a recent collection of his essays, this epigram was quoted by the president of the club in introducing the speaker of the evening. It is perhaps now the best known of Colonel Higginson's many sharp sayings; it is better known probably than his assertion that the American has " a drop more of nervous fluid " than the Englishman—an assertion which Matthew Arnold failed to understand but did not fail to denounce. No doubt it is hard for a writer as witty as Colonel Higginson to find one or two of his acute sentences quivering in the public memory, while others as well aimed fall off idly. But it is with the epigram as with the lyric; we shoot an arrow in the air, it falls to earth we know not where; and we can rarely foretell which shaft is going to split the willow wand.

Colonel Higginson need not be ashamed to go down to posterity as the author of one phrase, for many a writer is saved from oblivion by a single apothegm; nor need he be afraid of this fate, for there are "good things" a-plenty in this new volume, and some of them are certain to do good service in international combat, and to go hustling across the Atlantic again and again. There is an arsenal of epigram in the little essay called "Weapons of Precision," and it is pleasant to see that their effective range is more than 3000 miles. At that distance they have already wounded Mr. Andrew Lang, and forced from him a cry of pain. So sensitive did Mr. Lang show himself to these transatlantic darts that he allowed himself to reveal his ignorance of Colonel Higginson's work, of the Peabody Museum, and of various other men and things in America—a knowledge of which was a condition precedent to debate on the question.

This question is very simple: Is there such a man as an American? Has he ever done anything justifying his existence? Or is he simply a second-rate, expatriated Englishman, a colonist who is

to say ditto forever and a day? If we are
only debased duplicates of the Poor Isl-
anders, then our experiment here is a
failure, and our continued existence is not
worth while. If we are something other
than English, then it may be as well to
understand ourselves, and to throw off
any lingering bond of colonialism. This
is what Colonel Higginson's book was
intended to help us to do. " Nothing is
further," he has said in his preface, from
his " wish than to pander to any petty national vanity," his sole desire being to as-
sist in creating a modest and reasonable
self-respect. " The Civil War bequeathed
to us Americans, twenty-five years ago, a
great revival of national feeling; but this
has been followed in some quarters, during the last few years, by a curious relapse
into something of the old colonial and
apologetic attitude." No doubt this attitude is not characteristic of the best; it
is to be seen only in the East—chiefly in
New York and in Boston—chiefly among
the half-educated, for the man of wide
culture looks for light rather to Paris
and Berlin than to London.

Colonel Higginson proves abundantly,
with a cloud of witnesses, that one of the

differences between the American and the Englishman is the former's greater quickness. We are lighter and swifter in our appreciation of humor, for example. Indeed, it is amusing to observe that we speak of the English as obtuse in humor, just as they speak of the Scotch. I think that Colonel Higginson succeeds also in showing that there is greater fineness of taste in literature and in art in America; at least we do not take our dime novels seriously, while in England the leading weekly reviews really consider the stories of Miss Marryat and of Mr. Farjeon.

Of course "the added drop of nervous fluid" must be paid for somehow; in all international comparisons the great law of compensations holds good. Recently a leading American scientist told me that he thought there was, in American scientific work, a lack of the energy he had observed in the English. It was of pure science he was speaking; as far as applied science is concerned, there seems to be no lack of energy visible in the United States. That this criticism is just I cannot deny, having no wish to fall into the pitfall of discussing a subject of which I have no knowledge whatever. But if there is a possible loss of energy, there is an indisputable gain in mental flexibility, in openness of mind. There are Philistines in the United States, as there are in Great Britain, a many of them on both sides of the Atlantic ; but between the British Philistine and the American there is an essential difference. The British Philistine knows not the light, and he hates it and he refuses to receive it. The American Philistine knows not the light, but he is not hostile, and he is not only ready to receive it, but eager. This is a difference which goes to the root of the matter.

I have delayed so long over the subject of Colonel Higginson's book that I have now no space to speak of its style or of its separate chapters. " Weapons of Precision " I have already praised ; it is a protest against vulgarity of style—against the bludgeon and the boomerang as arms of debate ; it is a series of swift, rapierlike thrusts, to be considered by all who think that our language is inferior to the French in point and in brilliancy. Indeed, the whole book may be commended to those who can enjoy style and wit and learning and a knowledge of the world and a wisdom derived from men as well as from books. Especially may the essays on the "Shadow of Europe," on the "Perils of American Humor," on the "Evolution of an American," and on the "Trick of Self-Depreciation" be recommended to all who are downcast about the position of literature and of the arts in these United States, or about the United States as a nation. These essays are tonic and stimulant; and if their Americanism may seem to some aggressive, this is a failing which might become more common than it is without becoming dangerous—if always it were characterized by knowledge as wide as Colonel Higginson's and by wit as keen.

To no one may I venture to recommend Colonel Higginson's book more urgently than to Miss Agnes Repplier, who has sent forth a second volume of her entertaining magazine articles grouped under the excellent title of *Points of View*. Miss Repplier is very clever and very colonial. Although a Philadelphian, she has apparently never heard of the Declaration of Independence. From the company she keeps it is perhaps not an unfair inference to suggest that she seems to be sorry that she is not herself a Poor

Islander. She is a well-read woman, with all literature open before her, yet she quotes almost altogether from the contributors to the contemporary British magazines; and we feel that if birds of a feather flock together we have here in the eagle's nest by some mischance hatched a British sparrow.

Miss Repplier's subjects are excellent —"A Plea for Humor," "Books that Have Hindered Me," "Literary Shibboleths," "Fiction in the Pulpit," and the like; and she discusses them with ready humor and feminine individuality. She quotes abundantly and often aptly—and apt quotation is a difficult art. But the writers from whom she quotes are not always of that compliment. Bagehot had the gift of the winged phrase, and a quotation from his masculine prose is always welcome. But a glance down the list of the others from whom Miss Repplier quotes will show that she mischooses often. She seems to lack the sense of literary perspective; and for her one writer is apparently as good as another —so long as he is a contemporary Englishman.

There is no index to Miss Repplier's

book, but I have found amusement in making out a hasty list of those from whom she quotes. I do not vouch for its completeness or for its absolute accuracy, but it will serve to show that she is more at home in Great Britain than in the United States, and that her mind travels more willingly in the little compartments of a British railway carriage than in the large parlor cars of her native land. Besides Bagehot she cites Mr. Lang, Mr. Birrell, Mr. Shorthouse, Mr. Frederic Harrison, Mr. Radford, Mr. Swinburne, Mr. George Saintsbury, Mr. Gosse, Mr. James Payn, Mr. Ruskin, Mr. Pater, Mr. Froude, Mr. Oscar Wilde, and Miss "Vernon Lee." There is also one quotation from Doctor Everett, and one more from Doctor Holmes, or perhaps two. But there is nothing from Lowell, than whom a more quotable writer never lived. In like manner we find Miss Repplier discussing the novels and characters of Miss Austen and of Scott, of Dickens, of Thackeray, and of George Eliot, but never once referring to the novels or characters of Hawthorne. Just how it was possible for any clever American woman to write nine essays in criticism, rich in references and quotations, without once happening on Lowell or on Hawthorne, is to me inexplicable.

Colonialism is scarcely an adequate explanation for this devotion to the first-rate, second-rate, and third-rate writers of a foreign country to the neglect of the first-rate writers of her own. Perhaps the secret is to be sought rather in Miss Repplier's lack of literary standards. In literature as in some other things a woman's opinion is often personal and accidental; it depends on the way the book has happened to strike her; the angle of reflection is equal to the angle of incidence. Miss Repplier fails to apprehend the distinction between the authors who are to be taken seriously and the writers who are not to be taken seriously—between the man of letters who is somebody and the scribbler who is merely, in the French phrase, *quelconque*—nobody in particular. There is no need to go over the list of the persons from whom Miss Repplier quotes, and with whose writings she seems to have an equal familiarity; certain names on it are those of comic personalities not to be accorded the compliment of serious criticism.

Despite Miss Repplier's reliance on those British authors who have come to America to enlighten us with lectures in words of one syllable—to borrow a neat phrase of Colonel Higginson's—her *Points of View* are well chosen, and the outlook from them is pleasant. She writes brightly always, and often brilliantly. She does herself injustice by her deference to those whom she invites to her board, for she is better company than her guests. Her criticism one need not fully agree with to call it generally sensible and well put, and sometimes necessary. Perhaps her best pages contain her protest against critical shams and literary affectations. She has no patience with the man who, while really liking Mr. Haggard's tales of battle, murder, and sudden death, absurdly pretends to a preference for Tolstoï and Ibsen, whom his soul abhors. She has pleasant humor in her remark that those who read *Robert Elsmere* nowadays would think it wrong to enjoy *Tom Jones*, while the people who enjoyed *Tom Jones*—when it first came out—would have thought it wrong to read *Robert Elsmere;* and "that the people who, wishing to be on the safe side of virtue, think it wrong to read either, are scorned greatly as lacking true moral discrimination."

A bias in favor of one's own country-men is absurd when it leads us to accept native geese for swans of Avon ; but even then it is more creditable than a bias in favor of foreigners. So it is to be hoped that some of Miss Repplier's Philadel-phian friends will take her to Independ-ence Hall next Fourth of July and show her the bell that proclaimed liberty throughout the land. Then, on their way home, they might drop into a book-store and make Miss Repplier a present of Colo-nel Higginson's *The New World and the New Book*, and of Mr. Henry Cabot Lodge's *Studies in History* (wherein is to be found his acute account of " Colonial-ism in America "), and also of that volume of Lowell's prose which contains the fa-mous essay " On a Certain Condescension in Foreigners."

1892

## I.—OF MARK TWAIN'S BEST STORY

THE boy of to-day is fortunate indeed, and, of a truth, he is to be congratulated. While the boy of yesterday had to stay his stomach with the unconscious humor of *Sandford and Merton*, the boy of to-day may get his fill of fun and of romance and of adventure in the *Story of a Bad Boy*, in *Treasure Island*, in *Tom Brown*, and in *Tom Sawyer*, and then in the sequel to *Tom Sawyer*, wherein Tom himself appears in the very nick of time, like a young god from the machine. Sequels of stories which have been widely popular are not a little risky. *Huckleberry Finn* is a sharp exception to the general rule of failure. Although it is a sequel, it is quite as worthy of wide popularity as *Tom Sawyer*. An American

critic once neatly declared that the late
G. P. R. James hit the bull's-eye of success with his first shot, and that forever
thereafter he went on firing through the
same hole. Now this is just what Mark
Twain has not done: *Huckleberry Finn* is
not an attempt to do *Tom Sawyer* over
again. It is a story quite as unlike its predecessor as it is like. Although Huck Finn
appeared first in the earlier book, and although Tom Sawyer reappears in the
later, the scenes and the characters are
otherwise wholly different. Above all, the
atmosphere of the story is different. *Tom
Sawyer* was a tale of boyish adventure in
a village in Missouri, on the Mississippi
River, and it was told by the author.
*Huckleberry Finn* is autobiographic; it is
a tale of boyish adventure along the Mississippi River told as it appeared to Huck
Finn. There is not in *Huckleberry Finn*
any one scene quite as funny as those in
which Tom Sawyer gets his friends to
whitewash the fence for him, and then
uses the spoils thereby acquired to attain
the highest distinction of the Sunday-
school the next morning. Nor is there any
situation quite as thrilling as that awful
moment in the cave when the boy and the

girl are lost in the darkness; and when
Tom Sawyer suddenly sees a human hand
bearing a light, and then finds that the
hand is the hand of Indian Joe, his one
mortal enemy. I have always thought
that the vision of the hand in the cave in
*Tom Sawyer* was one of the very finest
things in the literature of adventure since
Robinson Crusoe first saw a single foot-
print in the sand of the sea-shore.

But though *Huckleberry Finn* may not
quite reach these two highest points of
*Tom Sawyer*, the general level of the later
story is indisputably higher than that of
the earlier. For one thing, the skill with
which the character of Huck Finn is
maintained is marvellous. We see everything through his eyes—and they are his
eyes, and not a pair of Mark Twain's
spectacles. And the comments on what
he sees are his comments—the comments
of an ignorant, superstitious, sharp, healthy
boy, brought up as Huck Finn had been
brought up; they are not speeches put
into his mouth by the author. One of
the most artistic things in the book—and
that Mark Twain is a literary artist of a
very high order all who have considered
his later writings critically cannot but

confess—one of the most artistic things
in *Huckleberry Finn* is the sober self-re-
straint with which Mr. Clemens lets Huck
Finn set down, without any comment at
all, scenes which would have afforded the
ordinary writer matter for endless moral
and political and sociological disquisition.
I refer particularly to the accounts of
the Grangerford - Shepherdson feud, and
of the shooting of Boggs by Colonel Sherburn.  Here are two incidents of the rough
old life of the South-western States and
of the Mississippi Valley, forty or fifty
years ago, of the old life which is now
rapidly passing away under the influence
of advancing civilization and increasing
commercial prosperity, but which has not
wholly disappeared even yet, although a
slow revolution in public sentiment is
taking place.  The Grangerford - Shepherdson feud is a vendetta as deadly as
any Corsican could wish, yet the parties
to it were honest, brave, sincere, good
Christian people, probably people of deep
religious sentiment.  None the less we see
them taking their guns to church, and,
when occasion serves, joining in what is
little better than a general massacre.  The
killing of Boggs by Colonel Sherburn is

told with equal sobriety and truth ; and the later scene in which Colonel Sherburn cows and lashes the mob which has set out to lynch him is one of the most vigorous bits of writing Mark Twain has done.

In *Tom Sawyer* we saw Huckleberry Finn from the outside; in the present volume we see him from the inside. He is almost as much a delight to any one who has been a boy as was Tom Sawyer. But only he or she who has been a boy can truly enjoy this record of his adventures and of his sentiments and of his sayings. Old maids of either sex will wholly fail to understand him, or to like him, or to see his significance and his value. Like Tom Sawyer, Huck Finn is a genuine boy ; he is neither a girl in boy's clothes, like many of the modern heroes of juvenile fiction, nor is he a " little man," a full-grown man cut down ; he is a boy, just a boy, only a boy. And his ways and modes of thought are boyish. As Mr. F. Anstey understands the English boy, and especially the English boy of the middle classes, so Mark Twain understands the American boy, and especially the American boy of the Mississippi Valley of forty or fifty years ago. The contrast between

Tom Sawyer, who is the child of respectable parents, decently brought up, and Huckleberry Finn, who is the child of the town drunkard, not brought up at all, is made distinct by a hundred artistic touches, not the least natural of which is Huck's constant reference to Tom as his ideal of what a boy should be. When Huck escapes from the cabin where his drunken and worthless father had confined him, carefully manufacturing a mass of very circumstantial evidence to prove his own murder by robbers, he cannot help saying, " I did wish Tom Sawyer was there; I knowed he would take an interest in this kind of business, and throw in the fancy touches. Nobody could spread himself like Tom Sawyer in such a thing as that." Both boys have their full share of boyish imagination; and Tom Sawyer, being given to books, lets his imagination run on robbers and pirates, having a perfect understanding with himself that, if you want to get fun out of this life, you must never hesitate to make believe very hard; and, with Tom's youth and health, he never finds it hard to make believe and to be a pirate at will, or to summon an attendant spirit, or to rescue a prisoner from the deepest dungeon 'neath the castle moat. But in Huck this imagination has turned to superstition; he is a walking repository of the juvenile folk-lore of the Mississippi Valley—a folk-lore partly traditional among the white settlers, but largely influenced by intimate association with the negroes. When Huck was in his room at night all by himself waiting for the signal Tom Sawyer was to give him at midnight, he felt so lonesome he wished he was dead:

"The stars was shining and the leaves rustled in the woods ever so mournful; and I heard an owl, away off, who-whooing about somebody that was dead, and a whippowill and a dog crying about somebody that was going to die; and the wind was trying to whisper something to me, and I couldn't make out what it was, and so it made the cold shivers run over me. Then away out in the woods I heard that kind of a sound that a ghost makes when it wants to tell about something that's on its mind and can't make itself understood, and so can't rest easy in its grave, and has to go about that way every night grieving. I got so downhearted and scared I did wish I had some company. Pretty soon a spider went crawling up my shoulders, and I flipped it off and it lit in the candle; and before I could budge it was all shrivelled up. I didn't need anybody to tell me that that was an awful bad sign and would fetch me some bad luck, so I was scared and most shook the clothes off me. I got up and turned around in my tracks three times and crossed my breast every time; and then I tied up a little lock of my hair with a thread to keep witches away. But I hadn't no confidence. You do that when you've lost a horseshoe that you've found, instead of nailing it up over the door, but I hadn't ever heard anybody say it was any way to keep off bad luck when you'd killed a spider."

And, again, later in the story, not at night this time, but in broad daylight, Huck walks along a road:

"When I got there it was all still and Sunday-like, and hot and sunshiny—the hands was gone to the fields; and there was them kind of faint dronings of bugs and flies in the air that makes it seem so lonesome like everybody's dead and gone; and if a breeze fans along and quivers the leaves, it makes you feel mournful, because you feel like it's spirits whispering—spirits that's been dead ever so many years—and you always think they're talking about *you*. As a general thing it makes a body wish *he* was dead, too, and done with it all."

Now, none of these sentiments are appropriate to Tom Sawyer, who had none of the feeling for nature which Huck Finn had caught during his numberless days and nights in the open air. Nor could Tom Sawyer either have seen or set down this instantaneous photograph of a summer storm :

" It would get so dark that it looked all blue-black outside, and lovely; and the rain would thrash along by so thick that the trees off a little ways looked dim and spider-webby; and here would come a blast of wind that would bend the trees down and turn up the pale underside of the leaves; and then a perfect ripper of a gust would follow along and set the branches to tossing their arms as if they was just wild; and next, when it was just about the bluest and blackest—fst ! it was as bright as glory, and you'd have a little glimpse of tree-tops a-plunging about, away off yonder in the storm, hundreds of yards further than you could see before ; dark as sin again in a second, and now you'd hear the thunder let go with an awful crash, and then go rumbling, grumbling, tumbling down the sky towards the under side of the world, like rolling empty barrels down-stairs, where it's long stairs and they bounce a good deal, you know."

The romantic side of Tom Sawyer is shown in most delightfully humorous fashion in the account of his difficult devices to aid in the easy escape of Jim, a runaway negro. Jim is an admirably drawn character. There have been not a few fine and firm portraits of negroes in recent American fiction, of which Mr. Cable's Bras-Coupé in the *Grandissimes* is perhaps the most vigorous, and Mr. Harris's Mingo and Uncle Remus and Blue Dave are the most gentle. Jim is worthy to rank with these ; and the essential simplicity and kindliness and generosity of the Southern negro have never been better shown than here by Mark Twain. Nor are Tom Sawyer and Huck Finn and Jim the only fresh and original figures in Mr. Clemens's book ; on the contrary, there is scarcely a character of the many introduced who does not impress the

reader at once as true to life—and therefore as new, for life is so varied that a
portrait from life is sure to be as good as
new. That Mr. Clemens draws from life,
and yet lifts his work from the domain of
the photograph to the region of art, is
evident to any one who will give his writing the honest attention which it deserves. The chief players in *Huckleberry
Finn* are taken from life, no doubt, but
they are so aptly chosen and so broadly
drawn that they are quite as typical as
they are actual. They have one great
charm, all of them—they are not written
about and about; they are not described
and dissected and analyzed; they appear
and play their parts and disappear; and
yet they leave a sharp impression of in-
dubitable vitality and individuality.

1886

## II.—OF A NOVEL OF M. ZOLA'S

IN his most suggestive study of the
*Greek World Under Roman Sway*, wherein we find the feelings, the thoughts,
and the actions of those who lived in

the first century explained and eluci-
dated by constant references to similar states of feeling, thought, and action
still surviving among us who live in the
nineteenth century, Professor Mahaffy
expresses his belief that the *Golden Ass*
of Apuleius does not give a true picture
of the Greek life it purported to represent, but that it is rather a reflection of
the depravity of the Romans to whom it
was addressed; and then he adds these
shrewd suggestions, to be borne in mind
by all who ever consider the fiction of a
foreign country or of another century:
"We might as well charge all society in
France with being addicted to one form
of vice, because recent French fiction oc-
cupies itself almost exclusively with this
as the material for its plots. The society
for which such books are written must
have shown that they are to its taste; the
society which such books portray may be
wholly different and grossly libelled by
being made to reflect the vices of the author and his readers."

If French society were composed exclusively of the men and women who people
most of the Parisian romances of the past
fifteen or twenty years; if the inhabitants

of the cities were like the miserable creatures we see in M. Zola's *Pot-Bouille*, and
if the dwellers in the fields were like the
horrible wretches we see in M. Zola's *La
Terre*, the outlook of France would be
black indeed, for no country could exist
or should exist which was peopled by such
a gang of monsters. But any one who
knows French life, any one especially
who knows the life of the larger provincial
towns, knows that what M. Zola has represented as typical and characteristic is, in
reality, exceptional and abnormal. Probably there is no house in the whole of
Paris occupied by as corrupt a set of ten-
ants as those set before us in *Pot-Bouille;*
and certainly there is no village in the
whole of France wherein all the horrors
depicted in *La Terre* could possibly have
taken place. The fact is, the French like
to boast about vice as the British like
to boast about virtue. I should doubt if
there was any great difference in morals
between the upper society of Paris and of
London, except the overwhelming hypoc-
risy of the latter. Apparently M. Zola
has at last awakened to some consciousness of the false impression produced by
his work. *Le Rêve* was his attempt to

produce a novel fit for the class to which nearly all English novels are addressed.

In his recent study, *L'Argent*, there is a fairer balance than in his other books; there are decent people, kindly folk, men and women of honest hearts and willing hands. We have a cheerful glimpse of the home life of Mazaud, the stock-broker who commits suicide when he fails. The Jordans, husband and wife, are perhaps the pleasantest pair to be found in all M. Zola's novels. With the novelist's increasing fame, apparently, he is taking brighter views of humanity. And Madame Caroline, despite her lapse, might almost be called an honest woman, if this is not a paradox; she is a strong, wholesome, broad-minded creature, admirably realized. The goddess Lubricity, whom Matthew Arnold first named as the presiding deity of French fiction, is still worshipped in other parts of the book; and her worship is out of place in this book at least, for those who are seized with the lust for gain have little time for any other. For example, the whole story of Saccard's relations with the Baroness Sandorff is needlessly offensive and revolting; and at bottom it is essentially false. But there is a marked improvement of tone in *L'Ar-gent* over certain even of his later books, while the atmosphere is nowhere as foul as it was in most of his earlier novels.

There is no disputing that M. Zola is a man with a dirty mind—with a liking for dirt for its own sake. There is no disputing also that he is a novelist of most extraordinary fecundity and force. Of all the books I have read in the past ten years, I received the strongest impression from Zola's *Germinal* and from Ibsen's *Ghosts;* and I can still hear the cry for light, and the pitiful appeal of the son to the mother with which the latter closes; and I can still feel the chill wind which whistles across the dark plain in the opening pages of the former. There is in *L'Argent* the same power, the same splendid sweep, the same mighty movement, the same symbolic treatment of the subject, the same epic method. M. Zola thinks himself a naturalist; he has preached naturalism from the house-top; he is generally taken at his word and criticised as a naturalist, and as a fact he is not a naturalist at all. M. Zola is not one who sees certain things in life, and who ties them together with a loose thread of plot—although this is the naturalism he approves of. He has preached it, but he has never practised it. On the contrary, M. Zola picks out a subject and reads up and crams for it, and conceives it as a whole, and devises typical characters and characteristic incidents, and co-ordinates the materials he has thus laboriously accumulated into a harmonious work of art, as closely constructed as a Greek tragedy and moving forward towards the inevitable catastrophe with something of the same irresistible impulse. No novelist of our time is affected less by what he sees in nature than M. Zola; not one is more consciously artful.

This symbolic method of M. Zola's is shown in *L'Argent* almost as clearly as in *Germinal*, which I cannot help considering his greatest novel, despite its prolixity and the foulness of many of its episodes. As *Germinal* was the story of a coal-mine with a strike, so *L'Argent* is a story of a gigantic speculation on the stock exchange, treated in the same epic fashion, with typical characters and all the necessary incidents. Obviously the Union Générale suggested certain particular details of Saccard's Banque Universelle. Obviously also Baron Rothschild sat for the portrait of Gundermann. There is the same use of minor figures to personify the crowd, and themselves identifiable by some broad characteristic — Moser, the bear; Pellerault, the bull; Amadrin, the speculator who foolishly blundered into a successful operation, and who has wisely held his tongue ever since; and all these minor characters (and there is a host of them) serve as a chorus, help along the main action of the tale, comment upon it, and typify the throng of men and women who are at the periphery of any great movement. These little people are all vigorously projected; they are all adroitly contrasted one with another; they are all carried in the hand of the novelist and manœuvred with unfailing effect, with a power and a certainty which no other living novelist possesses.

That many readers should be bored by all of Zola's writing I can readily understand, for it is not always easy reading. That many more should be shocked by him is even more comprehensible, for he has a thick thumb and he makes dirty marks over all his work. That some even should be annoyed by M. Zola's

method or irritated by his mannerisms, I
can explain without difficulty. But what
I cannot comprehend is that any one
having read *Une Page d'Amour* or *Germinal* or *L'Argent* can deny that M. Zola
is a very great force in fiction. But there
are critics in Great Britain—and even in
the United States, where we are less
squeamish and less hypocritical—who refuse to reckon with M. Zola, and who pass
by on the other side. A man must be
strong of stomach to enjoy much of M.
Zola's fiction ; he must be feeble in perception if he does not feel its strength
and its complex art. M. Zola's strength
is often rank, no doubt, and there is a foul
flavor about even his most forcible novels,
which makes them unfit for the library
of the clean-minded American woman.
But in any exact sense of the word M.
Zola's novels are not immoral, as the
romances of M. Georges Ohnet are immoral, for example, or those of the late
Octave Feuillet. Yet they are not spoon-
meat for babes.

1891

THE reader of *Humphrey Clinker* — if that robust and sturdy British story has any readers nowadays, when the art of fiction has become so much finer and more subtile — will remember that little Tim Cropdale " had made shift to live many years by writing novels at the rate of £5 a volume ; but that branch of business is now engrossed by female authors," so Smollett goes on to tell us, "who publish merely for the propagation of virtue, with so much ease and spirit and delicacy and knowledge of the human heart, and all in the serene tranquillity of high life, that the reader is not only enchanted by their genius but reformed by their mórality." *Humphrey Clinker* was first published in 1771, the year of its author's death ; and the names of the women of England who were writing novels six-score years ago are now forgotten. How many of the insatiate devourers of fiction who feed voraciously on the paper-cover-ed volumes of the news-stand have ever heard of the *Memoirs of Miss Sidney Bid-*

*dulph* for example?  Yet Charles James
Fox called this the best novel of his age ;
and Doctor Johnson found great interest
in following the misadventures of Miss
Biddulph, and declared to the authoress
that he knew not if she had a right, on
moral principles, to make her readers suf-
fer so much.  The authoress of the *Memoirs of Miss Sidney Biddulph* was Fran-
ces Sheridan, now remembered only because she was the mother of the author
of the *School for Scandal.*

Mrs. Sheridan was an estimable woman,
and it was not to her that Smollett turned
the edge of his irony.  There were in his
day not a few fashionable ladies who, in
"the serene tranquillity of high life," told
stories that neither enchanted by their
genius nor reformed by their morality.
In most of the novels written by women
in the second half of the eighteenth century, the morality is but little more obvious than the genius.  Like the fashionable English novels of the first half of this
century, now as carefully forgotten as the
tales of Smollett's fair contemporaries,
the female fiction with which Little Tim
Cropdale found himself unable to com-
pete was a curious compound of bad

morals, bad manners, and bad grammar.
Although stories by female authors who
"publish merely for the propagation of
virtue" and for the gratification of their
own vanity are still to be found in London by any one who will seek on Mr. Mu-
die's shelves, the standard of female fiction has been greatly elevated in England
since Miss Austen put forth her first modest story.

Charlotte Brontë and George Eliot followed in due season; and it would not
now be possible to draw up a list of the
ten greatest British novelists without
placing on it the names of two or three
women, at the least. There are diligent
readers of fiction who would insist that the
name of Mrs. Oliphant should be inscribed
among the chosen few, by reason of certain of her earlier tales of Scottish life;
and there are others equally insistent that
the strange romances of the English lady
who calls herself a French expletive en-
title the name of "Ouida" to be placed on
the roll of the chosen few. Indeed, the
admiration of those who do admire this
lady's stories is so ardent and fervid that
I sometimes wonder whether the twen-
tieth century will not see a Ouida Society

for the expounding of the inner spiritual meaning of *Under Two Flags* and *Held in Bondage.*

In America, since the day when Susanna Rowson wrote *Charlotte Temple*, and more especially since the day when Mrs. Stowe wrote *Uncle Tom's Cabin*, no list of American novelists could fairly be drawn up on which nearly half the names would not be those of women—even when one of these names might seem to be that of a man—like Charles Egbert Craddock's, for example. Colonel Higginson recently deplored the oblivion into which we have allowed the wholesomely realistic fiction of Miss Sedgwick to fall; and it has been remarked that the vigorous New England tales of Rose Terry Cooke never met with the full measure of success they deserved. But the authoress of *Ramona*, the authoress of *That Lass o' Lowrie's*, the authoress of *Anne*, the authoress of *Faith Gartney's Girlhood*, the authoress of *Signor Monaldini's Niece*, the authoress of *John Ward, Preacher*, the authoress of the *Story of Margaret Kent*, the authoress of *Friend Olivia*, and the authoresses of a dozen or of a score of other novels which have had their day of vogue,

these ladies are able easily to prove that
the field of fiction is being cultivated dili-
gently by the women of America.

One of the cleverest novels recently
published by any American woman is
*The Anglomaniacs*, which came forth
anonymously, but which Mrs. Burton Harrison has since acknowledged. It is a
sketch only, a little picture of a corner of
life, hardly more than an impression, but
is brilliant in color and accurate in drawing. Limited as it is in scope and con-
tracted as is its framework, it strikes me
as the best reflection of certain phases of
New York life since the author of the
*Potiphar Papers* made fun of the Rever-
end Mr. Creamcheese. It echoes the talk
of those who

> "tread the weary mill
> With jaded step and call it pleasure still."

And, better yet, it suggests the feelings
which prompted the talk. At a recent
meeting of the Nineteenth Century Club,
Mr. Theodore Roosevelt called Mr. Ward
McAllister's *Society as I Found It* an
"exposure of the 400;" and certainly it
is difficult to believe that even 100 people
of fashion could be found anywhere in

New York as dull as those Mr. McAllister saw around him, as narrow-minded and as thick-witted. Mrs. Burton Harrison knows what is called Society quite as well as Mr. McAllister; and as she is a clever woman, those she sees about her are often clever also. The company of Anglomaniacs to which she invites our attention are not dullards, nor are they cads, even though an ill-natured philosopher might be moved to call them snobs. A good-natured philosopher would probably find them amusing; and he would make shift to enjoy their companionship, dropping easily into acquaintance and laughing with them quite as often as he laughed at them.

In these days, when hosts of honest people throughout the United States are reading with delighted awe long accounts of the manners and customs of a strange tribe of human creatures, the female of which is known as a " Society Lady " and the male as a "Clubman," it is pleasant to find novels of New York life written by ladies who move within the charmed circle of what is called Society, and who can write about the doings of their fellows simply and without either snobbish wonder or caddish envy. The authoress of *The Anglomaniacs* and the authoress of *Mademoiselle Réséda* see Society as it is, and they are not so dazzled by the unexpected glare that they need to put on sea-side spectacles to enable them to observe what is going on about them. It is an old saying that to describe well we must not know too well, for long knowledge blunts the edge of appreciation. But those who, having knowledge, seek rather to reveal than to describe, often render a more valuable service than the more superficial observers who offer us their first impressions. Something of this revelation of Society we find in Mrs. Harrison's brilliant sketch and in the stories of " Julien Gordon."

Thackeray complained that no British novelist had dared to describe a young man's life since Fielding wrote *Tom Jones;* and Mr. Henry James, praising George Sand, notes the total absence of passion in English novels. If this reproach is ever taken away from our fiction, it will be by some woman. Women are more willing than men to suggest the animal nature that sheathes our immortal souls; they are bolder in the use of the stronger emotions; they are more willing to suggest the possibilities of passion lurking all unsuspected beneath the placidity of modern fine-lady existence. Perhaps they are sometimes even a little too willing: as Mr. Warner reminded us not long ago, " it may be generally said of novelists, that men know more than they tell, and that women tell more than they know."

It is by slow degrees that woman forges forward and takes her place alongside man in the mastery of the fine arts. The Muses were all women, once upon a time, but those whom they visited were all men. The first art in which the woman made herself manifestly the equal of the man was the art of vocal music—or was it that of dancing? The daughter of Herodias was mistress of both accomplishments. Then in time woman divided the stage with man; the histrionic art was possessed by both sexes with equal opportunity; and who shall say that Garrick or Kean surpassed in power Mrs. Siddons or Rachel? Now prose fiction is theirs quite as much as it is man's; and when the *Critic* recently elected by vote the twenty foremost American women of letters, many more than half were writers of

novels. The readers of *Humphrey Clinker* did not foresee Jane Austen and George
Eliot and George Sand any more than little Tim Cropdale could.

1891

## IV.—OF TWO LATTERDAY HUMORISTS

" Whoever and wherever and however
situated a man is, he must watch three
things—sleeping, digestion, and laughing,"
said Mr. Beecher; and he added with
equal wisdom, "they are three indis-
pensable necessities. Prayers are very
well, and reading the Bible very well indeed ; but a man can get along without
the Bible, but he can't without the other
three things." When a man has a clear
conscience, good digestion ought to wait
on appetite ; and when he has a good
digestion and a clear conscience, he ought
to find it easy to sleep well. Yet as sleep
is the only true friend that will not come
at one's call, he may be wakeful despite
his pure heart and quiet stomach; and in
this case he may fairly resort to the Pat-
ent-office reports or the British comic
papers, than which

> " Not poppy, nor mandragora,
> Nor all the drowsy syrups of the world "

are more potent soporifics. Many of the
avowedly humorous publications of the
day are better as a cure for sleeplessness
than as a cause of laughter. Of all sad
words of tongue or pen none is sadder
than what is known in many a newspaper
office as " comic copy." Wit cannot be
made to order, and humor cannot be pur-
chased by the yard, with a discount if the
buyer takes the whole roll.

In the *History of Henry Esmond*—
more veracious than many a more pre-
tentious history of the reign of Queen
Anne and of a broader truth—Thackeray
speaks of the " famous beaux-esprits,"
who " would make many brilliant hits—
half a dozen in a night sometimes—but,
like sharp-shooters, when they had fired
their shot, they were obliged to retire under cover till their pieces were loaded
again and they got another chance at
their enemy." And this figure expresses
the exact fact; no wit is a breech-loader—
still less is he a repeating rifle capable of
discharging sixteen shots without taking
thought. The readiest man must have
time to reload and the most fertile must

lie fallow now and again. Richard Brins-
ley Sheridan, even when he had most
carefully prepared himself, did not spar-
kle in private conversation as he was able
to make his characters scintillate through
the long sittings of the scandalous college. If needs must and the devil drives
a poor wretch to crack jokes unceasingly,
then of necessity the edge of his wit will
not be as keen nor the strokes of his
humor as effective. And this is why the
conducting of a comic paper is like the
leading of a forlorn hope. Success can
scarcely be more than a lucky accident.
"'Tis not in mortals to command success," and if Cato and Sempronius were
joint editors of a comic weekly it may be
doubted whether they would even deserve it. Nor would the author of the
tragedy from which this last quotation is
taken have been a satisfactory office editor of a comic weekly, although he contributed to the *Spectator* the delightfully
and delicately humorous sketch of Sir
Roger de Coverley.

This is why the level of comic journalism is not as lofty as we could wish. This
is why we frequently find poor jokes even
in journals where every effort is made to

provide good jokes. The supply is not
equal to the demand, and the jokesmith
often has to set his wits to work when
the stock of raw material is running low.
*Punch* and *Puck* are the representative
comic weeklies of the two great branches
of the English-speaking race. *Punch* has
had a great past. It may even be ques-
tioned whether those who declare its de-
cadence do not exaggerate its former
merits almost as much as they do its
present failings. It is vaguely remembered that in *Punch* Hood published the
"Song of the Shirt" and Thackeray the
*Book of Snobs*, and Douglas Jerrold the
*Story of a Feather*, and it is often supposed that there was a time when all
the clever men of London contributed
their best things every week to *Punch*.
But one has only to turn over the leaves
of any of the earlier volumes of the British weekly to discover that if this ever
were the case, then the clever men of
London were a very dull lot. *Punch* is
very much the same now that it was in
the past. Hood contributed the "Song
of the Shirt," and nothing else; Douglas
Jerrold wrote the *Story of a Feather*—
but who reads Douglas Jerrold nowa-

days? A'Becket composed a *Comic History of England*, and the few of us who have read it to-day feel as Dickens felt at the time, that it is dull and machine-made. Thackeray wrote *Mr. Punch's Prize Novelists* and the *Snob Papers;* and Thackeray was the "Fat Contributor;" and there has been no one like Thackeray since he left the paper.

But the pictures of *Punch* are as good now as ever they were; perhaps, taking one week with another, they are better. And the letter-press is very much what it has always been—rhymes, jingles, puns in profusion, topical allusions—"comic copy," in short. Now and then there is something in *Punch* which is still worth reading. There were Artemus Ward's papers a score of years ago, for instance, and there were more recently some of Mr. F. C. Burnand's earlier parodies and some of his earlier *Happy Thoughts*. Decidedly the most amusing prose which has appeared in *Punch* during the past four or five years is the series of overheard conversations called *Voces Populi*.

The author of *Voces Populi* is the " F. Anstey" who is well known in America as the writer of *Vice Versa* and of the

*Tinted Venus.* It is an open secret that the real name of "F. Anstey" is Guthrie, just as everybody knows that the real name of "Mark Twain" is Clemens. (The conjunction of these names was fortuitous, but it serves to remind me that I once heard Mr. Robert Louis Stevenson say that the two strongest chapters in the fiction of the past ten years were to be found, one in the *Giant's Robe* of "F. Anstey" and the other in the *Huckleberry Finn* of "Mark Twain.") The first book of an unknown author has small chance of sudden success, and *Vice Versa* was Mr. Guthrie's first book. Fortunately it came into the hands of Mr. Andrew Lang a few days after it was published, and Mr. Lang was so taken with its freshness, its truthfulness to boy nature, and its almost pathetic humor that he wrote a column about it in the *Daily News*—a column of the heartiest appreciation. "It was Lang's review that made the success of *Vice Versa*," said Mr. Guthrie to me once in London, two or three years ago, when we were planning to write a story together. And it was Mr. Lang who afterwards introduced the author of *Vice Versa* to the staff of *Punch.*

In *Voces Populi* Mr. Guthrie has gathered a score and a half of fragmentary dialogues, casual, plotless, but never pointless. They are thumbnail sketches of British character, "At a Dinner Party," "At a Wedding," "At the French Play," "At a Turkish Bath," "In an Italian Restaurant," in "Trafalgar Square" during a demonstration, and in "A Show Place." They are photographic in their accuracy, making due allowance for humorous foreshortening. They hit off the foibles of fashionable frivolity; they depict with unfaltering exactness the inconceivable limitations and narrowness of the middle class; but where they are most abundantly and triumphantly successful is in the rendering of the lower orders of London. Mr. Guthrie has caught the cockney in the very act of cockneyism, and he has here pilloried him for all time, but wholly without bitterness or rancor. Mr. Guthrie knows his roughs, his ruffians, his house-maids, his travellers, "Third Class—Parliamentary," and his visitors to "An East-End Poultry Show;" he knows them through and through; he sees their weakness; and after all he is tolerant, he does not dislike them in his heart, he handles them as though he loved them. We confess his kindliness of touch, even though it moves us to no more friendly feeling of our own. " Vox populi, vox Dei," says the adage, as true as most adages; but these *Voces Populi*, if not " Voces diaboli," might at least be called to the witness-box by the devil's advocate. It is a terrible indictment of contemporary British manners that we hear in these conversations, humorous as they are; and the indictment is perhaps the severer in that it is wholly unconscious. It is quite unwittingly that Mr. Guthrie offers this evidence to prove the truth of Matthew Arnold's assertion that one could see in England "an aristocracy materialized and null, a middle class purblind and hideous, a lower class crude and brutal."

In this respect at least no greater contrast could be found to the *Voces Populi* of Mr. Guthrie, reprinted from the British *Punch*, than the *Short Sixes* of Mr. H. C. Bunner, reprinted from the American *Puck*. The impression with which one rises from the reading of Mr. Bunner's tales is as different as possible from that with which one rises from the reading of Mr. Guthrie's dialogues. In the one book we see the British selfish, brutal, narrow‑minded; and in the other we see the Americans lively, kindly, good‑humored. In each case the volume is made up of matter contributed week by week to a comic journal. If it be objected that the satirist is bound perforce to show the seamy side of human nature, the obligation ought to be equally respected on both sides of the Atlantic; and the fact is that Mr. Guthrie reports conversations which are very clever and very amusing, but which give us no liking for his fellow‑countrymen; whereas Mr. Bunner's men and women we are ready and glad to take by the hand, even if we do not take them all to our hearts. Look down the *dramatis personæ* of Mr. Bunner's thirteen stories, and even the old curmudgeon who befools the little parson of one of "The Two Churches of Quawket" has humor enough to save him from hatred, and the little parson himself is pitiful rather than contemptible. Neither Colonel Brereton's Aunty nor the mendacious and persuasive colonel is a character whom any American would cross the street to avoid—far from it.

And as for the pert young person who en-
gages in " A Sisterly Scheme," and who
is perhaps the most forward and objec-
tionable young woman of recent fiction,
where is the American who could object
to her? Where, indeed, is the American
who does not envy Muffets the fun of his
courtship and the joy of his marriage?

George Eliot in one of her novels tells
us that "a difference of taste in jests is a
great strain on the affections"—a profound truth. There is little hope of hap-
piness in a union where one party has a
highly developed sense of humor and the
other none at all. That is perhaps the
reason why so few international marriages
are happy. Certainly, the chief characteristic of the figures in Mr. Guthrie's little
dramas is their absence of humor, and one
of the chief characteristics of the people
in Mr. Bunner's prose comedies is their
abundance of humor. We laugh at the
speakers in *Voces Populi*, while we laugh
with the actors in *Short Sixes*. And
we find in Mr. Bunner's book an unfailing variety, an unflagging ingenuity
and an unforced humor, now rich and
now delicate. We are delighted by wit,
playful and incessant and never obtrusive.

We discover ourselves to be dissolved in laughter, and often it is "the exquisite laughter that comes from a gratification of the reasoning faculty," as George Eliot called it in one of her letters. Never is it laughter that we ever feel ashamed of; near the smile there is often a tear, hidden, and to be found only by those who seek. "The Tenor," for example, which may seem to some hasty readers almost farcical, is in reality almost tragic, in that the heroine sees the shattering of an ideal and stumbles over the clay feet of her idol. The "Love Letters of Smith" are broadly funny, if you choose to think them so, but I feel sorry for the reader who pays that clever sketch the tribute of careless laughter only.

Next, perhaps, to Mr. Bunner's firm grasp of character, to his delicate perception, to his keen observation, to his faculty of hinting a pathetic undercurrent beneath the flow of humor, comes his felicity in suggesting the very essence of New York. Only three of the thirteen little tales are supposed to happen in this great city, and these are, perhaps, not likely to be the most popular; but they are enough to show again what Mr.

Bunner had already revealed in the *Story of a New York House* and in the still uncollected *Ballads of the Town*, that he has a knowledge of this busy city possessed by no other American writer of fiction. It is knowledge not paraded in his pages, but it permeates certain of his characters. Take "The Tenor," for example. In that lively story the young girl, seeking out the being whom she has worshipped from afar, rashly ventures into the hotel where the singer and his wife live. She goes as a servant, and she has a chance interview with one of the employees of the house—"a good-looking, large girl, with red hair and bright cheeks." This young person sees the name "Louise Levy" on the heroine's trunk. "You don't look like a sheeny," she remarks promptly. "Can't tell nothin' about names, can you? My name's Slattery. You'd think I was Irish, wouldn't you? Well, I'm straight Ne' York. I'd be dead before I was Irish. Born here. Ninth Ward, an' next to an engine-house." Could anything be more intensely, impressively, essentially Manhattan than this little vignette framed in the doorway of a hotel?

There are those who choose to speak of

Mr. Bunner as a humorist, because he is the editor of *Puck*. He is a humorist, no doubt, and his humor will endure, for it is founded on observation and on an understanding of his fellow-man. But he is a poet—as a true humorist must be. Perhaps his best story is "Love in Old Clothes," in which the humor and the poetry are inextricably blended, and in which there is a pure tenderness of touch I cannot but call exquisite. And yet, perhaps, I do not like it as well as the vigorous sketch called the "Zadoc Pine Labor Union." This is an object-lesson in Americanism; it is a model of applied political economy. And Zadoc Pine himself is one of the most direct and manly characters who has stepped from real life into literature. He has gumption and he has grit; he is an American as Benjamin Franklin was an American, and as Abraham Lincoln was. He could think as straight as he could shoot; and the tale of his rise in life is as potent a plea for freedom as Mr. Herbert Spencer's.

But about Mr. Bunner's writings I confess that I can never speak with the expected coldness of the critic, for the author is my friend for now many years. We have dwelt beneath the same roof for months at a time. We have exchanged counsel day and night; we have heard each other's plans and projects; we have read each other's manuscript; we have revised each other's proof-sheets; more than once we have written the same story together, he holding the pen, or I, as chance would have it. But shall friendship blind me to the quality of my comrade's art? When he puts forth a book, shall I pass by on the other side, silent, and giving no sign? That may be the choice of some, but it is not mine.

1891

# HARPER'S
# AMERICAN ESSAYISTS.

AMERICANISMS AND BRITICISMS, with
Other Essays on Other Isms. By BRANDER
MATTHEWS. With Portrait. 16mo, Cloth,
Ornamental, $1 00.

FROM THE BOOKS OF LAURENCE
HUTTON. With Portrait. 16mo, Cloth,
Ornamental, $1 00.

"Some American Book Plates," "Grangerism and
the Grangerites," "The Portraits of Mary Queen of
Scots," "Portrait Inscriptions," and "Poetical Inscriptions and Dedications" are the topics chosen by Mr.
Hutton, and the reader gets pleasure even as he gets
culture from a perusal of his studies in these fields.—
*Hartford Courant.*

CONCERNING ALL OF US. By THOMAS
WENTWORTH HIGGINSON. With Portrait.
16mo, Cloth, Ornamental, $1 00.

Colonel Higginson has the advantage of a sound and
simple philosophy of life to show off his fine literary
culture. The one makes him worth reading—strong,
open-minded, and wholesome ; the other gives him graces
of form, style, and literary attraction in great variety.
It is hard to decide whether the charm or the usefulness
of the present collection of essays preponderates.—*Independent,* N. Y.

[OVER]

### FROM THE EASY CHAIR. By GEORGE WILLIAM CURTIS. With Portrait. 16mo, Cloth, Ornamental, $1 00.

The essays have lost nothing of their actuality; their freshness of humor; their contagion of cheerful philosophy; their breathing, historical interest; their wit, that fits like a cap on Wisdom's head; their tenderness of humanity.—*Philadelphia Ledger.*

### AS WE WERE SAYING. By CHARLES DUDLEY WARNER. With Portrait, and Illustrated by H. W. MCVICKAR and Others. 16mo, Cloth, Ornamental, $1 00.

Mr. Warner possesses the faculty of putting his thoughts into excellent English, while the simplicity of his style, the absence of all straining after effect, and the apparently spontaneous character of his wit, sufficiently account for the high reputation he enjoys among the American humorists.—*Episcopal Recorder*, Philadelphia.

### CRITICISM AND FICTION. By WILLIAM DEAN HOWELLS. With Portrait. 16mo, Cloth, Ornamental, $1 00.

Many a good thing and many a true thing is here clothed in the diction of a master, and giving forth the bouquet of a style as delicately vigorous, so to say, as any in English literature.—*Independent*, N. Y.

**Published by HARPER & BROTHERS, New York.**

☞ *The foregoing works are for sale by all booksellers or will be sent by the publishers, postage prepaid, to any part of the United States, Canada, or Mexico, on receipt of the price.*